Literature Anthology

Level 5

**Siegfried Engelmann
Jean Osborn
Steve Osborn
Leslie Zoref**

A Division of The McGraw·Hill Companies

Columbus, Ohio

ACKNOWLEDGMENTS

Grateful acknowledgment is made to the following authors, agents, and publishers for permissions to use copyrighted materials:

Arizona Quarterly
"The Circuit" Reprinted from *Arizona Quarterly* Volume 29 (1973) by permission of the Regents of The University of Arizona.

Harcourt
"The No-Guitar Blues" from BASEBALL IN APRIL copyright © 1990 by Gary Soto, reprinted by permission of Harcourt, Inc.

Farrar, Straus and Giroux
"Thank You M'am" from SHORT STORIES by Langston Hughes. Copyright © 1996 by Ramona Bass and Arnold Rampersad. Introduction copyright © 1996 by Arnold Rampersad. Compilation and editorial contribution copyright © 1996 by Akiba Sullivan Harper. Reprinted by permission of Hill and Wang, a division Farrar, Straus and Giroux, LLC

Penguin Australia
"Without a Shirt" from UNREAL!: Eight Surprising Stories by Paul Jennings reprinted by permission of Penguin Books Australia Ltd.

Random House
"Like Jake and Me" Text copyright © 1987 by Mavis Jukes. Illustration copyright © 1987 by Lloyd Bloom. Reprinted by arrangement with Random House Children's Books, a division of Random House, Inc.

"Raymond's Run" by Toni Cade Bambara, copyright © 1971 by Toni Cade Bambara, from GORILLA, MY LOVE by Toni Cade Bambara. Used by permission of Random House, Inc.

Simon & Schuster
"The Bracelet" Reprinted with the permission of Atheneum Books for Young Readers, an imprint of Simon & Schuster Children's Publishing Division from THE SCRIBNER ANTHOLOGY FOR YOUNG PEOPLE edited by Anne Diven. Copyright © 1976 Yoshiko Uchida.

www.sra4kids.com

SRA/McGraw-Hill
A Division of The McGraw·Hill Companies

Copyright © 2002 by SRA/McGraw-Hill.

All rights reserved. Except as permitted under the United States Copyright Act, no part of this publication may be reproduced or distributed in any form or by any means, or stored in a database or retrieval system, without the prior written permission of the publisher, unless otherwise indicated.

Send all inquiries to:
SRA/McGraw-Hill
8787 Orion Place
Columbus, OH 43240-4027

Printed in the United States of America.

ISBN 0-07-569168-X

3 4 5 6 7 8 9 RRW 06 05 04 03 02

TABLE OF CONTENTS

Hans in Luck.......... 1

The Bracelet................. 17

The Jacket...... 32

Ginger's Challenge.......... 48

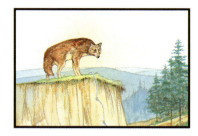
Brown Wolf............ 69

Like Jake and Me................ 88

TABLE OF CONTENTS (cont'd)

Thank You, M'am **103**

The Circuit **114**

Salmon Count **127**

The No-Guitar Blues **146**

Raymond's Run **157**

Without a Shirt **172**

Additional Reading **190**

…

Hans in Luck
The Brothers Grimm

New Vocabulary Words

1. exchange
2. peasant
3. fend
4. butcher
5. slaughter
6. remedy
7. trudge
8. vex
9. bargain
10. grindstone

Definitions

1. When you **exchange** something, you trade one thing for another thing.
2. A **peasant** is a person who lives and works on a farm.
3. When you **fend** for yourself, you take care of yourself.
4. A **butcher** is a person who kills animals and cuts meat.
5. When people **slaughter** animals, they kill the animals.
6. A **remedy** is a solution to a problem.
7. A person who is **trudging** is walking in a tired way.
8. If a person is **vexed** with you, he or she is annoyed with you.
9. A **bargain** is a good deal.
10. A **grindstone** is a flat stone used to polish and sharpen blades.

Story Background

"Hans in Luck" is a type of story called a folktale. Many folktales are old stories people told aloud. Parents would tell these stories to their children, and when the children became parents themselves, they would tell the same stories to their own children. Some stories were passed on in this way for hundreds of years without ever being written down.

In the early 1800s, two brothers from Germany named Jacob and Wilhelm Grimm began listening to folktales and writing them down. The folktales they collected were from Germany and other countries in Europe. Many of these folktales were hundreds of years old.

In the folktale you will read, Hans works as a servant for a master. Like many young people of that time, Hans had worked for his master for seven years. During that period, Hans had earned no money, but at the end of the seven years, his master pays Hans all his earnings in one payment. That payment is a lump of gold. The story tells what happens to Hans as he makes the long walk back to his mother's home with the lump of gold.

Focus Questions

- What is the value of the exchanges that Hans makes, beginning with the lump of gold?
- Why are the people Hans meets so interested in making exchanges with him?
- How did Hans feel at the end of the story?
- Why do you think the story is titled "Hans in Luck"?

Hans in Luck

The Brothers Grimm

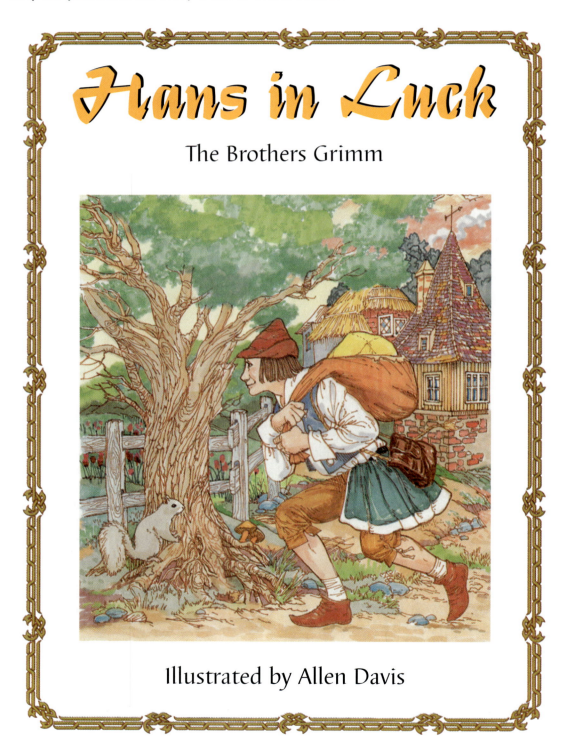

Illustrated by Allen Davis

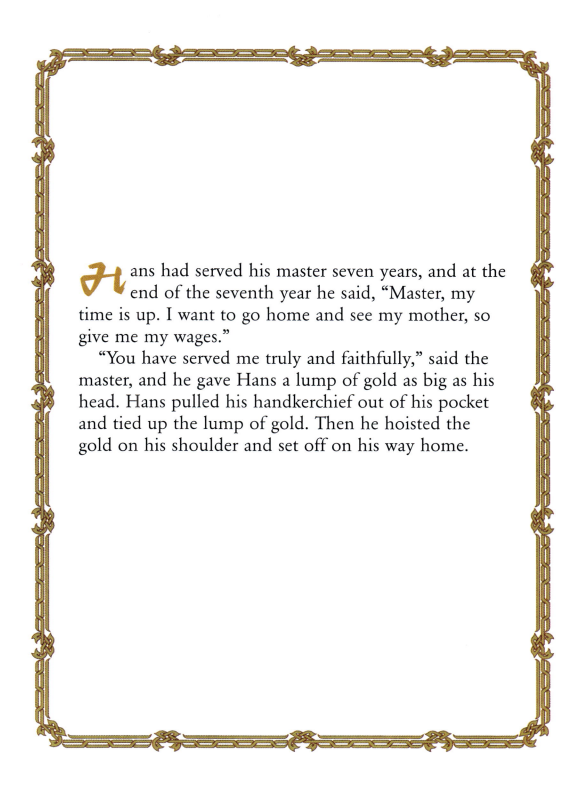

Hans had served his master seven years, and at the end of the seventh year he said, "Master, my time is up. I want to go home and see my mother, so give me my wages."

"You have served me truly and faithfully," said the master, and he gave Hans a lump of gold as big as his head. Hans pulled his handkerchief out of his pocket and tied up the lump of gold. Then he hoisted the gold on his shoulder and set off on his way home.

As Hans was trudging along, a man came riding by on a spirited horse, looking very lively. "Oh," cried Hans aloud, "how splendid riding must be! You sit at ease and don't stumble over stones."

The horseman heard Hans say this, and called out to him, "Well, what are you doing on foot?"

"I can't help myself," said Hans. "I have this great lump to carry. To be sure, it is gold, but then I can't hold my head straight because of it, and it hurts my shoulder."

"I'll tell you what," said the horseman, "we will trade. I will give you my horse, and you shall give me your lump of gold."

"Yes," said Hans. "But I warn you, you will find it heavy." And the horseman got down, took the gold, and, helping Hans up, he gave the reins into his hand.

"When you want to go fast," said he, "you must click your tongue and cry 'Gee-up!'"

And Hans, as he sat upon his horse, was glad at heart and rode off with merry cheer. After a while he thought he should like to go quicker, so he began to click with his tongue and to cry "Gee-up!" The horse began to trot, and Hans was thrown before he knew what was happening. There he lay in the ditch by the side of the road. The horse was caught by a peasant who was passing that way and driving a cow before him.

Hans pulled himself together and got upon his feet, feeling very vexed. "Riding is a poor business," said he, "especially on a mount like this, who starts off and throws you before you know where you are going. Never shall I try that game again. Now, your cow is something worth having. One can jog comfortably after her and have her milk, butter, and cheese every day, as part of the bargain. What would I not give to have such a cow!"

"Well now," said the peasant, "since it will be doing you such a favor, I don't mind exchanging my cow for your horse."

Hans agreed most joyfully, and the peasant, swinging himself into the saddle, was soon out of sight.

Hans went along driving his cow quietly before him, and thinking all the while of the fine bargain he had made.

"With only a piece of bread I shall have everything I can possibly want, for I shall always be able to add butter and cheese to it. And if I am thirsty I have nothing to do but to milk my cow. What more is there for a heart to wish?"

And when he came to an inn he made a stop. He ate up all the food he had brought with him, and bought half a glass of milk with his last two pennies. Then he went on again, driving his cow toward the village where his mother lived.

It was now near the middle of the day, and the sun grew hotter and hotter. Hans began to feel very hot, and so thirsty that his tongue stuck to the roof of his mouth.

"Never mind," said Hans, "I can find a remedy. I will milk my cow at once." And tying her to a tree, and taking off his leather cap to serve for a pail, he began to milk, but not a drop came. And as he set to work rather awkwardly, the impatient beast gave him such a kick on the head with her hind foot that Hans fell to the ground. For some time he could not think where he was. Luckily a butcher came by wheeling along a young pig in a wheelbarrow.

"This is terrible," cried the butcher, helping poor Hans on his legs again. Then Hans related to him all that had happened. The butcher handed him a jug of water, saying, "Here, take a drink, and you'll feel fine again. Of course the cow would give no milk, because she is old and only fit to pull burdens, or to be slaughtered."

"Well, to be sure," said Hans, scratching his head. "Who would have thought it? Of course it is a very handy way of getting meat when a man has a beast of his own to kill. But for my part I do not care much about beef, it is rather tasteless. Now, if I had but a young pig, that is much better meat, and then the sausages!"

"Look here, Hans," said the butcher, "just for love of you I will exchange. I will give you my pig instead of your cow."

"Heaven reward such kindness," cried Hans. Handing over the cow, he received in exchange the pig. The butcher lifted the pig out of the wheelbarrow and Hans led it away by a rope.

So on went Hans, thinking how everything turned out according to his wishes. After a while he met a peasant, who was carrying a fine white goose under his arm. They bid each other good-day, and Hans began to tell about his luck, and how he had made so many good exchanges. And the peasant told how he was taking the goose to a feast.

"Just feel how heavy it is," said the peasant, taking it up by the wings. "It has been fattening for the last eight weeks. When it is roasted, won't the fat run down."

"Yes, indeed," said Hans, weighing it in his hand, "very fine to be sure. But my pig is also desirable."

The peasant glanced cautiously on all sides of the animal and shook his head. "I am afraid," said he, "that there is something not quite right about your pig. In the village I have just left, a pig had actually been stolen from the sheriff's yard. I fear you have it in your hand. They have sent after the thief, and it would be a bad situation if the pig was found with you. At the least, they would throw you into a dark hole."

Poor Hans grew pale with fright. "For heaven's sake," said he, "help me out of this scrape. I am a stranger in these parts. Take my pig and give me your goose."

"It will be running some risk," answered the man, "but I will do it so you won't experience grief." And so, taking the rope in his hand, he drove the pig quickly along a by-path, and lucky Hans went on his way home with the goose under his arm.

"The more I think of it," said he to himself, "the better the bargain seems. First I get the roast goose and then the fat. That will last a whole year for bread and dripping. And lastly, I can stuff my pillow with the beautiful white feathers. How comfortably I shall sleep upon my pillow, and how pleased my mother will be."

And when he reached the last village, he saw a knife grinder. As the knife grinder's wheel went whirring round, he sang:

*My scissors I grind, and my wheel I turn,
And all good fellows my trade should learn,
For all that I meet with just serves my turn.*

Hans stood and looked at him. At last Hans said, "You seem very well off, and merry with your grinding."

"Yes," answered the knife-grinder, "my handiwork pays very well. I call a man a good grinder who finds money every time he puts his hand in his pocket. But where did you buy that fine goose?"

"I did not buy it. I exchanged it for my pig," said Hans.

"And the pig?"

"That I exchanged for a cow."

"And the cow?"

"That I exchanged for a horse."

"And the horse?"

"I gave for the horse a lump of gold as big as my head."

"And the gold?"

"Oh, that was my wage for seven years' service."

"You seem to have fended very well for yourself," said the knife-grinder. "Now, if you could have money in your pocket every time you put your hand in, your fortune would be made."

"How shall I manage that?" said Hans.

"You must be a knife-grinder like me," said the man. "All you want is a grindstone, and the rest comes of itself. I have one here. To be sure, it is a little damaged, but I don't mind letting you have it in exchange for your goose. What do you say?"

"How can you ask?" answered Hans. "I shall be the luckiest fellow in the world. If I find money whenever I put my hand in my pocket, there is nothing more left to want."

And so he handed over the goose to the knife-grinder and received a grindstone in exchange.

"Now," said the knife-grinder, taking up a heavy common stone that lay near him, "here is another sort of stone that you can hammer out your old nails upon. Take it with you, and carry it carefully."

Hans lifted up the stone and carried it off with a contented mind. "I must have been born under a lucky star," cried he, while his eyes sparkled with joy. "I have only to wish for a thing and it is mine."

After a while he began to feel rather tired, because he had been on his legs since daybreak. He also began to feel rather hungry, for he had eaten up all he had. At last he could scarcely go on at all. He had to stop every few moments, for the stones weighed him down. He wished that he did not have to drag them along.

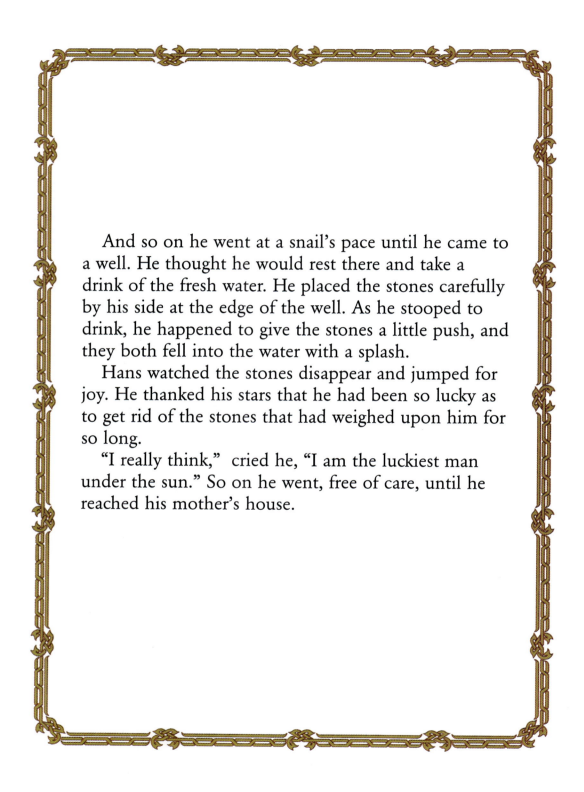

And so on he went at a snail's pace until he came to a well. He thought he would rest there and take a drink of the fresh water. He placed the stones carefully by his side at the edge of the well. As he stooped to drink, he happened to give the stones a little push, and they both fell into the water with a splash.

Hans watched the stones disappear and jumped for joy. He thanked his stars that he had been so lucky as to get rid of the stones that had weighed upon him for so long.

"I really think," cried he, "I am the luckiest man under the sun." So on he went, free of care, until he reached his mother's house.

Extending Comprehension

Story Questions

1. Make a list of the exchanges Hans made, beginning with "He exchanged the lump of gold for a horse."
2. Tell why the people Hans met were so interested in making exchanges with him.
3. Why did Hans think exchanging the gold for the horse was a good idea?
4. Why did Hans feel lucky at the end of the story?
5. Why do you think the story is titled "Hans in Luck"?
6. What do you think Hans's mother said about his exchanges when he got home?

Discussion Topics

1. This story can be interpreted in different ways. In one interpretation, Hans is unlucky because he keeps giving up valuable things until he ends up with nothing. In another interpretation, Hans is lucky because he gets rid of all the things that were a burden to him.

   Discuss these two interpretations with your classmates. During your discussion, try to answer the following questions:

   - Which interpretation do you agree with? Why?
   - Do you have another interpretation of the story? If so, what is it?

2. This story tells about people who make exchanges to get the things they want. With your classmates, discuss how you might get some things you want. During your discussion, try to answer the following questions:

   - What types of things would you like to get?
   - What kind of exchanges could you make to get those things?

3. People who are **gullible** believe everything they hear. It is easy to trick **gullible** people.

   With your classmates, decide if *gullible* is a word that you should use to describe Hans. During your discussion, try to answer the following questions:

   - Do the exchanges Hans makes make him appear gullible? Explain your answers.
   - Do Hans's statements make him sound gullible? Give some examples.

Writing Ideas

1. Write out the conversation that Hans and his mother might have when Hans arrives home. Have Hans explain what happened on his journey. Tell what his mother says as she listens to his story.
2. Pretend that you could have any one of the things Hans had, including the lump of gold, the horse, the cow, the pig, the goose, the grindstone, or the freedom from care. Which would you choose? Explain what you would do with your choice. Tell why you chose that thing.

The Bracelet

by Yoshiko Uchida
Illustrated by Karen Jerome

New Vocabulary Words

1. evacuated
2. concentration camp
3. interned
4. loyal
5. register
6. abandoned
7. bayonets
8. barracks
9. cots

Definitions

1. When families are **evacuated** by the government, they are forced to leave their homes and are taken to a different place to live.
2. A **concentration camp** is like a prison where large groups of innocent people are forced to stay.
3. When you are **interned,** you are taken to a place against your will and are not allowed to leave.
4. When you are **loyal** to your country, you support and defend the ideas your country stands for.
5. When you **register** somewhere, you give your name and important information about yourself.
6. When you feel **abandoned,** you feel completely alone and sad because someone you love has left you and is not coming back.
7. **Bayonets** are weapons that look like short swords. Bayonets are attached to the ends of guns.
8. **Barracks** are a group of large buildings where many people—usually soldiers—sleep.
9. **Cots** are thin, portable beds. Soldiers sleep on cots in their barracks.

Story Background

"The Bracelet" is an example of historical fiction. It is based on the experiences of Japanese Americans living on the West Coast of the United States during World War II. On December 7, 1941, the country of Japan bombed Pearl Harbor, Hawaii without any warning. Pearl Harbor was a very important base for the United States Navy, and many ships and lives were destroyed. The next day, the United States declared war against Japan.

Because of the war, the United States government questioned the loyalty of Japanese Americans who were living in America. The United States government thought Japanese Americans might help Japan attack the United States, so the government forced over 100,000 Japanese Americans to move to relocation camps. The author of the story you will read calls these places concentration camps.

The United States government considered important Japanese American community and business leaders to be especially dangerous; it called them enemy aliens. (Aliens are people who are not from the country in which they are living.) The leaders who were identified as enemy aliens were the first Japanese Americans the government interned, but they were sent to prisoner-of-war (POW) camps instead of relocation camps. When the war ended, the Japanese Americans were permitted to leave all these camps. Sadly, most of them no longer had homes or businesses to return to. Many years later, the United States government paid money to all living Japanese Americans who had been interned. The money was a small way for the government to apologize to its loyal citizens.

Focus Questions
- Why is Laurie's present so important to Ruri?
- How is Ruri's life at the concentration camp different from her life in Berkeley?
- What lesson does Ruri learn from her mother?

The Bracelet
by Yoshiko Uchida
Illustrated by Karen Jerome

"Mama, is it time to go?"

I hadn't planned to cry, but the tears came suddenly, and I wiped them away with the back of my hand. I didn't want my older sister to see me crying.

"It's almost time, Ruri," my mother said gently. Her face was filled with a kind of sadness I had never seen before.

I looked around at my empty room. The clothes that Mama always told me to hang up in the closet, the junk piled on my dresser, the old rag doll I could never bear to part with; they were all gone. There was nothing left in my room, and there was nothing left in the rest of the house. The rugs and furniture were gone, the pictures and drapes were down, and the closets and cupboards were empty. The house was like a gift box after the nice thing inside was gone; just a lot of nothingness.

It was almost time to leave our home, but we weren't moving to a nicer house or to a new town. It was April 21, 1942. The United States and Japan were at war, and every Japanese person on the West Coast was being evacuated by the government to a concentration camp. Mama, my sister Keiko and I were being sent from our home, and out of Berkeley, and eventually, out of California.

The doorbell rang, and I ran to answer it before my sister could. I thought maybe by some miracle, a messenger from the government might be standing there, tall and proper and buttoned into a uniform, come to tell us it was all a terrible mistake; that we wouldn't have to leave after all. Or maybe the messenger would have a telegram from Papa, who was interned in a prisoner-of-war camp in Montana because he had worked for a Japanese business firm.

The FBI had come to pick up Papa and hundreds of other Japanese community leaders on the very day that Japanese planes had bombed Pearl Harbor. The government thought they were dangerous enemy aliens. If it weren't so sad, it would have been funny. Papa could no more be dangerous than the mayor of our city, and he was every bit as loyal to the United States. He had lived here since 1917.

When I opened the door, it wasn't a messenger from anywhere. It was my best friend, Laurie Madison, from next door. She was holding a package wrapped up like a birthday present, but she wasn't wearing her party dress, and her face drooped like a wilted tulip.

"Hi," she said. "I came to say good-bye."

She thrust the present at me and told me it was something to take to camp. "It's a bracelet," she said, before I could open the package. "Put it on so you won't have to pack it." She knew I didn't have one inch of space left in my suitcase. We had been instructed to take only what we could carry into camp, and Mama had told us that we could each take only two suitcases.

"Then how are we ever going to pack the dishes and blankets and sheets they've told us to bring with us?" Keiko worried.

"I don't really know," Mama said, and she simply began packing those big impossible things into an enormous duffel bag—along with umbrellas, boots, a kettle, hot plate, and flashlight.

"Who's going to carry that huge sack?" I asked.

But Mama didn't worry about things like that. "Someone will help us," she said. "Don't worry." So I didn't.

Laurie wanted me to open her package and put on the bracelet before she left. It was a thin gold chain with a heart dangling on it. She helped me put it on, and I told her I'd never take it off, ever.

"Well, good-bye then," Laurie said awkwardly. "Come home soon."

"I will," I said, although I didn't know if I would ever get back to Berkeley again.

I watched Laurie go down the block, her long blond pigtails bouncing as she walked. I wondered who would be sitting in my desk at Lincoln Junior High now that I was gone. Laurie kept turning and waving, even walking backwards for a while, until she got to the corner. I didn't want to watch anymore, and I slammed the door shut.

The next time the doorbell rang, it was Mrs. Simpson, our other neighbor. She was going to drive us to the Congregational church, which was the Civil Control Station where all the Japanese of Berkeley were supposed to report.

It was time to go. "Come on, Ruri. Get your things," my sister called to me.

It was a warm day, but I put on a sweater and my coat so I wouldn't have to carry them, and I picked up my two suitcases. Each one had a tag with my name and our family number on it. Every Japanese family had to register and get a number. We were Family Number 13453.

Mama was taking one last look around our house. She was going from room to room, as though she were trying to take a mental picture of the house she had lived in for fifteen years, so she would never forget it.

I saw her take a long last look at the garden that Papa loved. The irises beside the fish pond were just beginning to bloom. If Papa had been home, he would have cut the first iris blossom and brought it inside to Mama. "This one is for you," he would have said. And Mama would have smiled and said, "Thank you, Papa San," and put it in her favorite cut-glass vase.

But the garden looked shabby and forsaken now that Papa was gone and Mama was too busy to take care of it. It looked the way I felt, sort of empty and lonely and abandoned.

When Mrs. Simpson took us to the Civil Control Station, I felt even worse. I was scared, and for a minute I thought I was going to lose my breakfast right in front of everybody. There must have been over a thousand Japanese people gathered at the church. Some were old and some were young. Some were talking and laughing, and some were crying. I guess everybody else was scared too. No one knew exactly what was going to happen to us. We just knew we were being taken to the Tanforan Racetracks, which the army had turned into a camp for the Japanese. There were fourteen other camps like ours along the West Coast.

What scared me most were the soldiers standing at the doorway of the church hall. They were carrying guns with mounted bayonets. I wondered if they thought we would try to run away, and whether they'd shoot us or come after us with their bayonets if we did.

A long line of buses waited to take us to camp. There were trucks, too, for our baggage. And Mama was right; some men were there to help us load our duffel bag. When it was time to board the buses, I sat with Keiko and Mama sat behind us. The bus went down Grove Street and passed the small Japanese food store where Mama used to order her bean-curd cakes and pickled radish. The windows were all boarded up, but there was a sign still hanging on the door that read, "We are loyal Americans."

The crazy thing about the whole evacuation was that we were all loyal Americans. Most of us were citizens because we had been born here. But our parents, who had come from Japan, couldn't become citizens because there was a law that prevented any Asian from becoming a citizen. Now everybody with a Japanese face was being shipped off to concentration camps.

"It's stupid," Keiko muttered as we saw the racetrack looming up beside the highway: "If there were any Japanese spies around, they'd have gone back to Japan long ago."

"I'll say," I agreed. My sister was in high school and she ought to know, I thought.

When the bus turned into Tanforan, there were more armed guards at the gate, and I saw barbed wire strung around the entire grounds. I felt as though I were going into a prison, but I hadn't done anything wrong.

We streamed off the buses and poured into a huge room, where doctors looked down our throats and peeled back our eyelids to see if we had any diseases. Then we were given our housing assignments. The man in charge gave Mama a slip of paper. We were in Barrack 16, Apartment 40.

"Mama!" I said. "We're going to live in an apartment!" The only apartment I had ever seen was the one my piano teacher lived in. It was in an enormous building in San Francisco with an elevator and thick carpeted hallways. I thought how wonderful it would be to have our own elevator. A house was all right, but an apartment seemed elegant and special.

We walked down the racetrack looking for Barrack 16. Mr. Noma, a friend of Papa's, helped us carry our bags. I was so busy looking around, I slipped and almost fell on the muddy track. Army barracks had been built everywhere, all around the racetrack and even in the center oval.

Mr. Noma pointed beyond the track toward the horse stables. "I think your barrack is out there."

He was right. We came to a long stable that had once housed the horses of Tanforan, and we climbed up the wide ramp. Each stall had a number painted on it, and when we got to 40, Mr. Noma pushed open the door.

"Well, here it is," he said, "Apartment 40."

The stall was narrow and empty and dark. There were two small windows on each side of the door. Three folded army cots were on the dust-covered floor and one light bulb dangled from the ceiling. That was all. This was our apartment, and it still smelled of horses. Mama looked at my sister and then at me. "It won't be so bad when we fix it up," she began. "I'll ask Mrs. Simpson to send me some material for curtains. I could make some cushions, too, and … well …" She stopped. She couldn't think of anything more to say.

Mr. Noma said he'd go get some mattresses for us. "I'd better hurry before they're all gone." He rushed off. I think he wanted to leave so that he wouldn't have to see Mama cry. But he needn't have run off, because Mama didn't cry. She just went out to borrow a broom and began sweeping out the dust and dirt. "Will you girls set up the cots?" she asked.

It was only after we had put up the last cot that I noticed my bracelet was gone. "I've lost Laurie's bracelet!" I screamed. "My bracelet's gone!"

We looked all over the stall and even down the ramp. I wanted to run back down the track and go over every inch of the ground we'd walked on, but it was getting dark and Mama wouldn't let me.

I thought of what I'd promised Laurie. I wasn't ever going to take the bracelet off, not even when I went to take a shower. And now I had lost it on my very first day in camp. I wanted to cry.

I kept looking for it all the time we were in Tanforan. I didn't stop looking until the day we were sent to another camp, called Topaz, in the middle of a desert in Utah. And then I gave up.

But Mama told me never mind. She said I didn't need a bracelet to remember Laurie, just as I didn't need anything to remember Papa or our home in Berkeley or all the people and things we loved and had left behind.

"Those are things we can carry in our hearts and take with us no matter where we are sent," she said.

And I guess she was right. I've never forgotten Laurie, even now.

Extending Comprehension

Story Questions

1. How did Ruri feel about leaving her home? Give an example from the story that supports your answer.
2. Name at least two reasons why you think Laurie's present was so important to Ruri.
3. Describe at least three different things Ruri observed when she reached her new home, Apartment 40.
4. How did Ruri's mother react when she was faced with difficult situations?
5. Why do you think the author never had Ruri find her bracelet?

Discussion Topics

1. What did Ruri's mother mean when she said, "Those are things we carry in our hearts and take with us no matter where we are sent"?

   During your discussion, try to answer the following questions:

   - What valuable lesson did Ruri learn when she lost the bracelet Laurie had given her?
   - Can you give an example from your own life of "things you carry in your heart"?

2. Do you think the United States government did the right thing when it interned Japanese Americans during the war?

   During your discussion, try to answer the following questions:

   - What were some reasons for internment of the Japanese Americans?
   - What were some reasons against internment of the Japanese Americans?

Writing Ideas

1. Pretend you are Ruri. Write a letter to Laurie describing your experiences at Barrack 16, Apartment 40. Tell where you live and how you feel. Be sure to include all the parts of a friendly letter.
2. What do you think was the worst part of Ruri's internment? Explain your answer.

STORY 3
AFTER LESSON 30

The Jacket
by Steven Otfinoski
Illustrated by Anthony Accardo

New Vocabulary Words

1. customary
2. bewildered
3. aroused
4. flustered
5. fret

6. candidate
7. election
8. podium
9. improvise
10. philosophical

11. expectant
12. ovation
13. landslide
14. frankly
15. potential

Definitions

1. **Customary** is another way of saying *usual*.
2. **Bewildered** is another way of saying *confused*.
3. **Aroused** is another way of saying *awakened*.
4. **Flustered** is another way of saying *nervous*.
5. When you **fret,** you worry.
6. A **candidate** is a person who is running for office.
7. During an **election,** people vote for the candidates who are running for office.
8. A **podium** is a piece of furniture that a speaker stands behind.
9. When you **improvise,** you do not prepare ahead of time to do something, you just do it.
10. If you feel **philosophical** about something that happened, you accept what happened, even though you may not be happy about it.
11. When you are expecting something to happen, you may have an **expectant** expression on your face.
12. An **ovation** is loud applause that lasts a long time. When the audience stands and applauds, it is called a standing ovation.
13. When you win an election by a **landslide,** you win by a lot of votes.
14. **Frankly** is another way of saying *honestly*.
15. When you realize your **potential,** you become what is possible for you to be.

Story Background

"The Jacket" is a modern fable about self-confidence and the power we each have inside of us. Walter is a "nerdy" student until he gets a magical jacket. When the jacket disappears, Walter is very worried. By the end of the story, you will find out what Walter learns about himself.

Focus Questions

- How does wearing the jacket make Walter feel?
- How are things different for Walter after he starts wearing the jacket?
- Do you think the jacket is a magical jacket?

The Jacket
by Steven Otfinoski
Illustrated by Anthony Accardo

My name is Walter, I'm in the sixth grade, and until a few weeks ago, I was the number one nerd at school. Then I put on the jacket and everything changed. But I think I'd better start at the beginning. Otherwise, I'm sure you won't believe what happened to me. I can hardly believe it myself.

It all started one Friday during lunch period. I was standing in line in the school cafeteria when "Gorilla" Gordon walked up to me. His real name is Gus, but everyone calls him Gorilla because he looks and acts like one. Of course, most kids only call him that behind his back. You live longer that way.

"Hi, punk," Gorilla said. "How about moving aside and letting me ahead of you? I'm really hungry today."

"Sure, Gus," I smiled. "Go right ahead."

To add insult to injury, Gorilla stomped on my foot as he walked past. It hurt, but I didn't say a word. Besides being a nerd, I was a coward, too.

After getting my lunch, I sat down at a table next to the new kid in school. His name is Bob and he's a pretty nice guy. At least he didn't get up and leave when I sat down next to him like the other kids do.

"Why do you take that stuff from that big ape?" Bob asked me. He had seen what happened in line.

"Simple," I replied. "If I didn't, he'd cream me."

"He's not so tough," said Bob. "If you only stood up to him, I bet he'd crumble in a minute."

I wasn't enjoying this conversation at all and wished I'd taken my customary seat at an empty table. "That's easy for you say," I told Bob. "You're bigger. Guys like Gorilla don't pick on you."

"Size doesn't have anything to do with it," replied Bob. "It's all in how you see yourself. I think I know someone who can help you."

Bob reached into his pocket, pulled out a small white business card, and handed it to me. I read the fine black print.

I looked up at Bob, bewildered. "I don't need any new clothes," I told him.

Bob just grinned. "Yes, you do," he said. "Mr. Calducci helped me, and he can help you too."

It sounded crazy, but I had to admit Bob had aroused my curiosity. So Saturday morning I hopped on my bike and pedaled down to River Road.

Calducci's Clothing Shop certainly wasn't much to look at. The shop window was dirty, and the sign above it looked as if it would fall apart if you breathed on it. But then I saw it in the window—the most awesome jacket I had ever laid eyes on. It was made of black leather with fringe the colors of the rainbow and beaded cuffs. Across the back in glowing letters were written the words "KING OF THE MOUNTAIN."

"Like to try it on?" someone spoke quietly. I looked up and saw a balding, middle-aged man with a black mustache. He was standing in the doorway. "Are you Mr. Calducci?" I asked.

"That's me," he said smiling. "Come on inside and I'll show you the jacket."

I hesitated. "I'm sure it's too expensive for me," I mumbled.

"Let's not talk about money," said the man, ushering me into the store. "One thing at a time."

So I tried on the jacket. It was a perfect fit. This was strange, because in the window it looked several sizes bigger. My skin tingled when I put it on. It felt like there was a current of electricity running through me. It was exciting and a little scary at the same time.

"This jacket was made for you, young man," said Mr. Calducci.

"Maybe," I said, "but it wasn't made for my allowance. I'm sure I can't afford it."

"So, don't buy it," replied the store owner. "I'll tell you what. You can take it on loan."

I never heard of a clothing store loaning clothes, but I wasn't going to argue with him. "You mean like a rental?" I asked.

"Yes, something like that," said Mr. Calducci. "See how you like it and we'll talk later."

I thanked him and left wearing the jacket.

That night, I joked and talked at dinner more than I can ever remember. I actually felt completely at ease with my parents and we didn't have *one* argument. My parents even believed my story about the jacket! It was truly amazing. I couldn't explain it, but the new jacket gave me a confidence that I'd never felt before.

The next day I woke up feeling full of enthusiasm. I actually looked forward to going to school. That was a switch! I put on my jacket over my school clothes and looked in the mirror. I wondered what the other kids would think of it.

You might say my taste in clothes before this was definitely on the nerdish side. What I wore pretty much reflected my personality. No one seemed to notice me much, which is just the way I liked it.

But did they ever notice me now! I was the center of attention the moment I strolled into class. And the amazing part was I thoroughly enjoyed it!

Our teacher, Ms. Bateman, gave us a surprise quiz that morning. I normally get so flustered during quizzes that I automatically get half the answers wrong. Or else I fret so long over one question that I never finish in time. But not now. I felt cool as a cucumber in my new jacket and answered every question with ease. When Ms. Bateman returned the corrected quizzes just before lunchtime, I had a perfect 100.

"Good work, Walter," said Ms. Bateman. "I'm pleased to see your study habits are improving."

How could I tell her my study habits had nothing to do with it—that it was all the jacket's doing?

In the lunch line, everyone wanted to get a closer look at my jacket. Kids who never noticed I was alive before were suddenly treating me like their best friend. That's when Gorilla Gordon made his appearance.

"Where'd you get the cool threads, punk?" Gorilla sneered. "The Army and Navy Store?"

I looked at Gorilla and then at the other kids. No one said a word. I suddenly realized I wasn't scared of this bully one bit.

"Look, Gorilla," I said, looking him right in the eye, "why don't you find a nice tall tree to climb up into, and leave the jungle floor to us intelligent humans?"

You should've seen the expression on Gorilla's face! Once he got over the shock of having Walter the Nerd talk back to him, however, he got good and angry. He reached out and grabbed me by the front of my jacket.

Before I knew what I was doing, I pulled his hands away and flipped him over my shoulder. He let out a groan as he hit the floor and just lay there stunned for a moment.

The circle of students cheered. "Guess that'll teach you to mess with the king!" yelled one boy.

Gorilla got up to the sound of jeering laughter, gave me a nasty look, and stalked away. That day I didn't have any problem finding company for lunch. Nearly everyone wanted to sit at my table and talk with me. In one day, I had gone from being Mr. Nobody to the Personality Kid.

At one point, I glanced up and saw Bob sitting across at another table. I smiled at him and he winked back at me. We were the only two people in school who knew the secret of my success.

From then on, I wore my jacket everywhere. At school, at home. I even slept in it. I quickly became the best student in my class and the top athlete on the playing field during recess. Everyone was my friend—everybody but Gorilla Gordon—and when the time came to elect a class president for all the sixth grades, I was the leading candidate.

The day before the election was to be held, each candidate was supposed to give a short speech in a special assembly. I wrote my speech the night before. (It was brilliant, of course!) When I'd finished, I folded the speech and put it in my jacket pocket.

The next morning at school, all my friends were congratulating me as if I had already won the election. Before the assembly, I took my place backstage with the other three candidates.

Ms. Bateman asked me if I'd carry the wooden speakers' podium from backstage to center stage. It must have weighed fifty tons, and it was tough trying to lift it with my jacket on. So I took off the jacket and carefully folded it over a chair backstage. Then I lugged the podium out to the middle of the stage as the students took their seats in the auditorium.

Imagine my surprise when I came backstage and found my jacket was gone! Who could've taken it? I immediately thought of Gorilla Gordon. This was his revenge for showing him up in the cafeteria that day! I had to find him and get it back.

But just then Ms. Bateman appeared. "We're ready to begin, Walter," she said. "You'll speak second, all right?"

"But I can't," I stammered.

"What do you mean?" asked the teacher.

"My jacket's gone!" I told her.

"It is?" she said. "Maybe you just misplaced it. I'm sure it's around here someplace."

"You don't understand," I said. "My speech was in the pocket of my jacket."

"Oh," said Ms. Bateman. "Well, I'm sure you can improvise. You're such an excellent public speaker."

Now, the King of the Mountain was an excellent public speaker. But without that jacket, I wasn't king of anything. The moment of truth had come.

"Well," I said to myself, trying to be philosophical, "it was fun while it lasted."

The first candidate finished her speech. Ms. Bateman gave me the signal to come out on stage. That twenty-foot walk to the podium was the longest walk of my life.

I gazed out over the expectant faces of my classmates. They looked eager, anxious to hear what I was going to say. Just realizing they already liked me, even before I opened my mouth, was comforting. Maybe all wasn't lost yet, I thought to myself.

"Fellow students," I began at last. "You've all noticed a big change in me over these past few weeks. Well, it wasn't really me that changed, but the way I felt about myself. My jacket says 'King of the Mountain.' I think we're all kings of the mountain in our own ways. Maybe all anyone needs is a little confidence to scale the mountain. If you elect me your class president, I'll make it my goal to help you reach the top. If we work together, I think we can make our school number one. Thank you."

That was it. Short and sweet. There was a long moment of silence. I really blew it, I thought to myself. Then suddenly the applause started. Everybody in the auditorium was clapping and shouting. Some kids were even giving me a standing ovation. It was incredible!

As I made way for the next speaker, I noticed Gorilla Gordon down in front, clapping right along with everyone else. He didn't look like someone who had just stolen my jacket, but then maybe he was a better actor than I thought.

That afternoon, I looked all over school for the jacket. But it was nowhere to be found. I went home a worried wreck. The next day at school I had even more reason to worry. The votes were counted and I won the election by a landslide. Now I really felt like a fake. How was I ever going to make good as class president without my jacket to give me confidence?

After class, I rushed down to River Road to Calducci's Clothing Shop. I figured whatever kind of wizard Mr. Calducci was, he could make me another jacket like the first one. But to my amazement, there was my jacket in the window where I had first seen it!

"Hello, young man," said Mr. Calducci when I entered the shop. "I'm surprised to see you back here."

"Not as surprised as I am," I told him. "How on earth did my jacket get back here?"

"That's simple," he explained. "I picked it up backstage before your speech. I told you it was only a loan."

I was stunned. "But why did you take it at the very moment I needed it most?"

Mr. Calducci smiled and shook his head. "You had no more use for it—as your speech proved. Frankly, I think it was a big improvement over the one you wrote. You made a discovery about yourself in that speech. The jacket was just a way to show you what you had inside all along."

It was beginning to sink in. Mr. Calducci was right. The jacket helped me to realize my potential. Now that I had confidence in myself, I didn't need it anymore.

"So the jacket always comes back to you?" I asked.

"Of course," he said. "All my clothes are strictly on short-term loan."

"I don't know how to thank you," I told him.

"The best way you can thank me is to tell someone else about my shop—someone else who needs a shot of self-confidence," said Mr. Calducci.

I said I would do that. Before I left, I took one last look at the jacket in the window. It didn't look so special anymore. It looked just like any other jacket.

That was a week ago. I haven't found anyone yet who needs Mr. Calducci's help. Maybe you know someone who could use a little self-confidence? Say, you look a little down in the dumps yourself. Why don't you take this card I have here? I know you won't be sorry…

Extending Comprehension

Story Questions

1. How did Walter feel about himself before he got the jacket?
2. How did wearing the jacket make Walter feel?
3. Name at least three things that were different for Walter after he started wearing the jacket.
4. Do you think the jacket had magical powers? Use evidence from the story to support your answer.
5. Mr. Calducci said that Walter discovered something about himself. What did Walter discover?

Discussion Topics

1. An old saying tells us that "you're only as good as you think you are."

   Discuss this saying with your classmates. During your discussion, try to answer the following questions:

   - How does this saying apply to Walter?
   - How does this saying apply to you?

2. The jacket plays an important role in this story; it is almost like a character.

   Discuss whether or not the jacket has magical powers.

   - What parts of the story make you think the jacket has magical powers?
   - What parts of the story make you think the jacket does not have magical powers?

3. This story ends with Walter offering Mr. Calducci's card to you. Why do you think the author ended the story this way?

   During your discussion, try to answer the following questions:

   - In what kinds of situations do most students need a little more confidence?
   - Do you like the way this story ended? Explain your answer.

Writing Ideas

1. Tell three things you would like to do if you had a jacket from Mr. Calducci's store. Also, tell how you would feel if you were wearing the jacket.
2. When you improvise, you are doing something without preparing to do it. When you are philosophical about something that happened, you accept what happened, even though you are not happy about it. Write about a time you had to improvise something. Or, write about a time you tried to be philosophical about something that happened to you.

**STORY 4
AFTER LESSON 40**

Ginger's Challenge

by Josephine Noyes Felts
Illustrated by Sandy Rabinowitz

New Vocabulary Words

1. rebellious
2. loafing
3. mounted up

4. barbed wire
5. tousled
6. smoldering

7. stile
8. cutoff
9. clapper
10. indignant

Definitions

1. When you are **rebellious,** you resist doing what you are asked to do.
2. When you are **loafing,** you are wasting time.
3. Things that are **mounting up** are piling up.
4. Wire fence with small sharp pieces sticking out is called a **barbed wire** fence.
5. When you look **tousled,** you look messy.
6. When a fire **smolders,** it burns with little smoke and no flame.
7. Steps that are built next to a wall or a fence are called a **stile**.
8. A **cutoff** is a shortcut.
9. The **clapper** of a bell is the piece of metal that makes a noise when it hits the bell.
10. **Indignant** is another word for *angry*.

Story Background

Many people are fascinated by the beauty and power of horses. And why not? Horses are fascinating animals. Long ago, people discovered that horses could be trained to do the kind of work that required strength and speed. Horses pulled the plows that farmers used to prepare the land for planting seeds. Horses pulled big wagons loaded with heavy supplies. A single horse could carry one person from one place to another much faster than that person could walk. Teams of horses pulled the big carriages and stagecoaches that carried people from one place to another. Knights in armor even rode horses into battles.

Horses are no longer needed to do this kind of work. Most farmers do not need horses to pull their plows. They use tractors to plow their fields and trucks to carry their supplies. People don't ride on horses or sit in horse-drawn carriages to get from one place to another. Instead, they use cars, buses, trains, and airplanes. Horses no longer carry knights in armor into battles.

In some places, however, horses still work for people. Men and women who work on cattle ranches use horses to help them round up cattle, and in some cities, police officers ride horses to help them direct crowds of people. But today, most horses are used for pleasure. Some people ride horses because they like to be outside riding on trails that go through fields and woods. Others train horses to compete in horse

This story was originally published as "The Winning of Dark Boy."

shows. Still other people train horses to run in races. You read about one kind of race in "A Horse to Remember."

Many writers have written stories about horses and about the people who take care of and ride horses. Some young people love horse stories and read as many of them as they can get their hands on. As they read these stories, they learn some of the special "horse" words that people who work with horses use and that writers like to use in the stories they write about horses. In "Ginger's Challenge," you will come across words that name the parts of a horse, words that describe how horses move, and words that name the equipment people use to control horses.

In the section below, some of these words are defined. Read these definitions before you start reading the story. You may also want to look back and read the definitions as you need them to help you better understand the story.

Some words that name parts of a horse:

- The **muzzle** is the front part of a horse's head.
- **Hooves** are the hard, tough coverings of the feet of a horse.
- The **flanks** are the sides of a horse.
- The **withers** are located between the horse's shoulder bones at the bottom of its neck.

Some words that describe how horses move:

- When a horse **prances,** it moves proudly and in a lively way.
- When a horse **bolts,** it suddenly runs away, sometimes because it has been frightened.
- When a horse **gallops,** it goes very fast.
- When a horse **canters,** it is going a little slower than a gallop.
- When a horse **rears,** it stands up on its hind legs.
- When a horse **throws off** a rider, it jumps up and down, or rears, so that the rider falls off the saddle.
- When a horse **shies,** it stops suddenly or moves away quickly because something has frightened it.

Some words that name equipment used to control horses:

- A **lunge line** is a long rope used to exercise a horse.
- A **harness** is the leather strap a horse wears when hitched to a cart or wagon.
- The **bridle** is the leather strap a horse wears on its head while being ridden or driven.
- The **reins** are the straps attached to the bridle that the rider uses to control the horse.
- The **saddle** is the leather seat that is strapped to the body of the horse. A rider sits on the saddle.
- The **stirrups** are made of metal and are attached by straps to the saddle. Riders place their feet in the stirrups.

Some other words used in stories about horses:

- When a horse is **tethered,** it is tied up with a short rope so that it can move only a short distance.
- A **horsewoman** is a woman who knows a lot about riding horses and who is a very good rider.
- When a rider wants her horse to jump, she leans forward, stands in the stirrups, and holds up her body. When she does this, she is **lifting to jump.** She does not interfere with the horse's movement as it jumps.
- Each time a rider and a horse go around a racetrack, they complete a **lap.**
- When a rider and a horse practice together, the horse gets a **workout.**

Focus Questions

- At the beginning of the story, why does Tommy talk about the barbed wire fence at the farm of Mr. and Mrs. Zigafoos?
- Why does Ginger decide to go for help?
- How does the author write about bad weather, and how does the bad weather make Ginger's trip even more difficult?
- Why does Ginger decide to take the cutoff?
- What are Ginger's doubts and worries as she rides to the village?

Ginger's Challenge

by Josephine Noyes Felts
Illustrated by Sandy Rabinowitz

"I don't believe it. I just don't believe it!" whispered Ginger Grey to herself as she watched Dark Boy, the beautiful black steeplechaser, going round and round on the lunge, the training rope to which he was tethered in the O'Malley's yard. She was stroking him with her eyes, loving every curve, every flowing muscle of his slender, shining body.

But the voice of Tim O'Malley, Dark Boy's owner, still echoed in her ears. "You're a brave little horsewoman, Ginger, but Dark Boy would kill you. I'm getting rid of him next week. He's thrown three experienced men and run away twice since I've had him. You are not to get on him!"

Ginger wiped a rebellious tear from her cheek, looking quickly around to make sure that neither ten-year-old Tommy nor the two younger children had seen her. She was alone at the O'Malley farm, several miles away from home, looking after the O'Malley children while their father and mother were in town. Why couldn't she have had the exercising and training of this glorious horse! Her heart ached doubly, for she longed to ride him next week in the horse show at Pembroke.

Ginger glanced now at the two little girls playing in the yard. They needed their noses wiped. She took care of this, patted them gently, and went back to where Dark Boy was loafing at the end of the lunge. He didn't seem to mind the light saddle she had put on him. The reins of the bridle trailed the ground. She must go soon and take it off. He'd had a good workout today, she thought with satisfaction. Exercise was what he needed. And now with nobody riding him . . .

She shivered suddenly and noticed how much colder it had turned. A great bank of black clouds had mounted up over the woods behind the meadow. She studied the clouds anxiously. Bad storms sometimes rose quickly out of that corner of the sky. The air seemed abnormally still, and there was a weird copper light spreading from the west.

If it was going to storm she'd better get the children in the house, put Dark Boy in the barn, and find Tommy. Here came Tommy now, dirty, tousled, one leg of his jeans torn and flapping as he walked.

"Barbed wire," he explained cheerfully, pointing to his pants. "Zigafoos has fenced his fields with it!"

A sharp gust of wind rounded the house. Tommy flapped in it like a scarecrow. A shutter on the house banged sharply; the barn door creaked shrilly as it slammed. Dark Boy reared and thudded to the ground.

"Look!" yelled Tommy suddenly. "What a close funny cloud!"

A thin spiral of smoke was rising from behind the O'Malley's barn. Ginger's heart froze within her. Fire! She raced around the barn. Then she saw with horror that the lower part of that side was burning. The wind must have blown a spark from a smoldering trash pile. Already the blaze was too much for anything she and Tommy could do. She'd have to get help at once!

As she tore back toward the house, pictures flashed through her mind. The big red fire truck was in the village six miles down the road. There were no phones. Any cars in the scattered neighborhood would be down in the valley with the men who used them to get to work at the porcelain factory. She'd have to get to the village and give the fire alarm herself immediately. Perhaps on Dark Boy . . .

She dashed over to him and caught his bridle. He tossed his head and sidled away from her, prancing with excitement. As she talked quietly to him, with swift fingers she loosened the lunge, letting it fall to the ground. She felt sure that she could guide him if only she could get on him and stay on him when he bolted. She thrust her hand deep in her pocket and brought out two of the sugar lumps she had been saving for him.

"Sugar for a good boy," she panted and reached up for his muzzle. Dark Boy lipped the sugar swiftly, his ears forward.

With a flying leap Ginger was up, had swung her right leg over him and slipped her right foot in the stirrup. She sat lightly forward as jockeys do. Would he resent her? Throw her off? Or could she stick?

Indignant, Dark Boy danced a wide circle of astonishment. The wind was whistling furiously now around the house, bending the trees. Ginger held the reins firmly and drew Dark Boy to a prancing halt. Then, suddenly, he reared. She clung with her lithe brown knees and held him tight. Precious minutes were flying. She thought of the bright tongues of flame licking up the side of the barn.

"Tommy! Take care of the children!" she shouted over her shoulder as Dark Boy angrily seized the bit between his teeth and whirled away. "I'll get help!"

Ginger's light figure in a red blob of sweater flashed down the road through the twisting trees. Fast as Dark Boy's bright hooves beat a swift rhythm on the hard clay road, Ginger's thoughts raced ahead. She glanced at her watch. By the road it was six miles to the town. At Dark Boy's throbbing gallop they might make it in fifteen minutes. By the time the fire department got back, it might well be much too late.

There was a crash like thunder off in the woods to her left as the first dead tree blew down. Dark Boy shied violently, almost throwing her headlong, but she bent lower over his neck and clung. Suddenly her heart stiffened with dread. What had she done! She'd been wrong to leave the children. Suppose Tommy took them into the house, and the house caught fire from the barn! She hadn't thought of the wind and the house. She'd only thought of saving the barn!

Desperately she pulled at Dark Boy's mouth. But he was going at a full runaway gallop, the bit between his teeth. Stop now? Go back? No!

There was one way that she might save precious seconds: take him across the fields, the short cut, the way the children went to school. That way it was only two miles! There were fences between the fields, but Dark Boy was a steeplechaser and trained to jump. She'd have to take a chance on jumping him now. They thundered toward the cutoff.

Peering ahead for fallen trees as the branches groaned and creaked above her, she guided him into the little lane that ran straight into a field where the main road turned sharply. Now he was responding to her touch, his great muscles flowing under his glossy coat like smoothly running water. She held him straight toward the stile at the far end of the field. Here was the place to take their first jump. Would he shy before it and make them lose the moments they were saving? Or would he take it smoothly?

She leaned anxiously forward and patted Dark Boy's silky neck. "Straight into it, beautiful! Come on, Boy!"

Dark Boy laid back an ear as he listened. A few yards ahead of the stile, she tightened the reins, lifted his head, and rose lightly in the stirrups. Dark Boy stretched out his neck, left the ground almost like a bird, she thought. His bright hooves cleared the stile.

"Wonderful, beautiful Boy!" Ginger cried as they thudded on.

Now to the second fence! Over it they went, smooth as silk. Her heart lifted.

Down below them in the valley the little town of Honeybrook flashed in and out of sight behind the tortured trees. She thought briefly of the steep bank from the lower field onto the road below. What would Dark Boy do there? Would he go to pieces and roll as horses did sometimes to get down steep banks? Or could she trust him, count on his good sense, hold him firmly while he put his feet together and slid with her safely to within reach of the fire alarm?

They were headed now across a rounded field. Dark Boy lengthened his glistening neck, stretched his legs in a high gallop. Just then, irrelevantly, Tommy flashed into Ginger's mind, his torn jeans flapping in the wind. "Barbed wire! Oh, Dark Boy!"

Here was a danger she had not considered, a danger that stretched straight across their path, one she could not avoid! The lower end of Zigafoos' field, the one they were crossing now at such headlong speed, was fenced with it. Dark Boy couldn't possibly see it! This time she would be helpless to lift him to the jump. He'd tear into it, and at this pace, he would be killed. She would never give her warning. Her heart beating wildly, she pulled the reins up to her chest.

"This way, Boy!" turning his head.

He curved smoothly. There weren't two of them now; horse and rider were one. They made the wide circle of the field. First at a gallop, then dropping to a canter and a walk. She stopped him just in time. He was quivering, shaking his head, only a few feet from the nearly invisible, vicious wire. As she slid to her feet, the wind threw her against him.

"Here, Boy, come on," she urged breathlessly. Dark Boy, still trembling, followed her. She skinned out of her sweater and whipped its brilliant red over the barbed wire, flagging it for him. "There it is, Boy, now we can see it!"

Dark Boy was breathing heavily. Without protest this time, he let her mount. She dug her heels into his flanks and put him into a gallop for the jump. Amid a thunder of hooves she took him straight for the crimson marker. Dark Boy lifted his feet almost daintily, stretched out his head, and they were clear!

He galloped now across the sloping field. "Good Boy, good Boy!" she choked, patting his foaming withers as he stretched out on the last lap of their race against fire and time.

The wind was still sharp in her face, but the terrifying black clouds had veered to the south, traveling swiftly down the Delaware valley. She could see distinctly the spire of the old church rising above the near grove of trees. How far beneath them it still seemed! That last fifty feet of the trail they would have to slide.

"Come on!" she urged, holding the reins firmly, digging her heels into his flanks to get one last burst of speed from his powerful frame. They flew along the ledge. Ahead in the clearing she could see the long bank that dropped to the road leading into the town. Just under top runaway speed but breathing hard, Dark Boy showed that the race was telling on him. With gradual pressure she began to pull him in.

"Slow, Boy, slow," she soothed. "You're doing fine! Don't overshoot the mark. Here we are, old fellow. Slide!"

His ears forward, his head dipped, looking down, quivering in every inch of his spent flanks, Dark Boy responded to the pressure of her knees and hands. Putting his four feet together, he half slid, half staggered down the bank and came to a quivering stop on the empty village street not ten feet from the great iron ring that gave the fire alarm. He was dripping and covered with foam.

As Ginger's hand rose and fell with the big iron clapper, the clang of the fire alarm echoed, and people ran to their doors. The alarm boomed through the little covered bridge up to Smith's machine shop. The men working there heard it, and dropping their tools, came running, not bothering to take off their aprons. It rang out across Mrs. Harnish's garden. Mr. Harnish and the oldest Harnish boy heard it and vaulted lightly over the fence, then ran, pulling on their coats.

While the big red engine roared out of the Holms' garage and backed up toward the canal bridge to get under way, Ginger called out the location of the fire. She fastened Dark Boy securely to a fence and climbed into the fire truck. They roared away up the hill.

Ginger looked at her watch again. In just eight minutes, she and Dark Boy had made their race through the storm. It seemed eight hours! A few more minutes would tell whether or not they had won.

"Please, God," Ginger whispered, "take care of Tommy and the girls!"

They slowed briefly at Erwin's corner to pick up two more volunteers, then sent the big red truck throbbing up Turtle Hill. Tears trickled down between Ginger's fingers. Ned Holm threw an arm gently around her shoulders.

"Good girl!" he said smiling at her reassuringly. "We go the hill up! We get there in time!"

Ginger shook the tears from her eyes and thanked him with a smile. But at the wheel Rudi set his lips in a grim line as he gave the truck all the power it had and sent it rocking over the rough road. The siren screamed fatefully across the valley. A barn can burn in little time and catch a house, too, if the wind is right, and this wind was right!

"How'd you come?" he growled.

"Across the fields—on Dark Boy."

"Dark Boy!" Rudi's eyes narrowed and he held them fixed on the road as he steered.

Ned Holm gasped. "You mean that steeplechaser nobody can stay on?"

"I stayed on!"

They rounded the turn at the top of the hill. Now they could see the great black cloud of smoke whirling angrily over the O'Malley's trees. As they came to a throbbing stop in the O'Malley's yard and the men set up the pump at the well, a corner of the house burst into flames. Five minutes more and . . . !

Tommy ran panic-stricken toward them. The barn was blazing fiercely now and in a little while all that would be left of it would be the beautiful Pennsylvania Dutch stonework. A stream of water played over the house. Sparks were falling thick and fast but the stream was soaking the shingles.

Ginger caught Tommy in her arms. "Where are the kids?" she shouted.

"In—in the house. I carried them up and then put the fence at the stairs. They don't like it much!"

Ned Holm ran with Ginger up the steep, narrow stairs and helped her carry out the squirming, indignant children.

That night when the fire was out and the big O'Malleys were home, and the little O'Malleys safely in bed, Ginger at home told her mother all about the day. She was a little relieved that nobody scolded her about riding Dark Boy. Her mother just cried a little and hugged her.

Next morning they saw Tim O'Malley riding Dark Boy up the Greys' lane. Ginger raced out to meet him. Tim swung down and led the black horse up to Ginger.

"Here's your horse," he said simply. "You've won him!"

Ginger stared at him speechless.

Tim went on. "I want you to ride Dark Boy next week in the Pembroke show. And I expect you to win!"

"We'll try, sir," said Ginger.

Extending Comprehension

Story Questions

1. At the beginning of the story, how did Ginger feel about Dark Boy? Support your answer with information from the story.
2. When Tommy O'Malley comes home from visiting Mr. and Mrs. Zigafoos' fields, he says his pants are torn because of the barbed wire. Why is the author telling you about that barbed wire fence?
3. List at least three things Ginger worries about as she rides Dark Boy to the village.
4. Why did Mr. O'Malley give Dark Boy to Ginger?

Discussion Topics

1. At the beginning of the story, Ginger's problem was that she wanted to ride Dark Boy but couldn't. She had another problem when the barn caught on fire. She had to decide what to do. Discuss how she resolved these two problems. Then think about the problem that was facing Dark Boy at the beginning of the story. During your discussion, try to answer the following questions:
   - What were the two problems that Ginger and Dark Boy faced at the beginning of the story?
   - How did Ginger resolve those two problems?
   - How did she and Mr. O'Malley resolve the problems of Dark Boy?
2. When Dark Boy was galloping to the village, he faced many challenges. Ginger, who was a good horsewoman, helped him meet those challenges. During your discussion, try to answer the following questions:
   - What were some of the challenges that Dark Boy faced in his race to the village?
   - What did Ginger do to help Dark Boy meet each one of his challenges?
3. While she was riding on Dark Boy to the village, Ginger had some worries and doubts about what she was doing. During your discussion, try to answer the following questions:
   - What were Ginger's worries and doubts about leaving the farm?
   - What would you do if you had to choose between going for help or staying with the children and watching the barn burn?

Writing Ideas

1. Find some of the "horse words" in the story and use as many of them as you can to write a description of a horse you would like to own. Or write an entire story about a horse.
2. In this story, Ginger faced an emergency. She chose to do something dangerous to get help. To carry out her decision, she had to leave the children in the house. She told their brother to take care of them. Do you think she did the right thing to ride away for help? Write her a letter explaining your answer.
3. The bad weather plays an important role in this story. In some places, the author uses vivid words and sentences to describe the bad weather. Find at least two places in which the author describes the weather. Write down some of her words and then write a paragraph that tells how those words helped you imagine what the weather was like in the story.
4. If you are particularly interested in horses, ask your teacher or your librarian to help you find more books about horses. You can start a horse dictionary that includes the words you read in "Ginger's Challenge" and "A Horse to Remember." When you read more books about horses, you can add more words to your horse dictionary.

Brown Wolf

by Jack London
Illustrated by Joel Snyder
adapted for young readers

STORY 5
AFTER LESSON 50

New Vocabulary Words

1. cottage
2. cliff
3. gliding effortlessly
4. spring

5. fangs
6. bristle
7. miracle
8. hardships

9. dog sounds:
   - snarl
   - bark
   - growl
   - cry
   - howl
   - whine
   - pant

Definitions

1. A **cottage** is a small house.
2. A **cliff** is a very steep side of a hill or mountain.
3. An animal that is running smoothly and easily is **gliding effortlessly.**
4. A **spring** is a place where fresh water comes out of the ground.
5. **Fangs** are the four pointed teeth that many animals have.
6. When a dog **bristles,** the fur on its back stands on end.
7. A **miracle** is an event that cannot be explained.
8. When you put up with difficulties, you put up with **hardships.**
9. **Dog sounds: Snarl, bark, growl, cry, howl, whine,** and **pant.**

Story Background

The author of "Brown Wolf," Jack London, was born in San Francisco, California, in 1876. His family was poor. He left school to earn money and find adventure. He worked on fishing boats in San Francisco Bay and then shipped out as a sailor on a ship that went to Japan. When he returned to the San Francisco Bay area, he decided to see his own country. He hitched rides on railroad trains and visited and worked in many parts of the United States.

He came back to the San Francisco area and went to high school. He was very smart, and he worked hard. He was able to do most of his four years of high school studies in one year. After that year, he went to the University of California and began to write stories about his travels. He left the university to travel to Alaska during the gold rush of 1897. The winter he spent there inspired much of his writing, including "Buck," the Jack London story you read in your textbook.

Jack London did not settle in one place for very long. He always wanted to visit new places. When he left Alaska, he went to England, to Russia, and then to the South Pacific. Everywhere he went, he wrote about what he saw and heard.

He finally settled in northern California. He bought land near a small town called Glen Ellen and built a house that he named "Wolf House." He wrote "Brown Wolf" while he was living in Glen Ellen. Because Jack London liked to write about where he was living, he wrote about the land surrounding Glen Ellen in this story. Jack London died in Glen Ellen in 1916. He was only forty years old, but he had written fifty books.

To better appreciate the strength of "Brown Wolf," you should know that the distance from the town of Glen Ellen to the southern border of Oregon is about 300 miles. You should also know that the state of Washington is another 250 miles from southern Oregon. Finally, the Yukon Territory is over 2,000 miles from Glen Ellen.

Focus Questions

- Who are the main characters in this story?
- What are the many things Marge and Walt do to win Wolf's love?
- What do we learn about Wolf that makes people think he is from the north?
- How does Wolf treat Skiff Miller? How does he treat other strangers?
- The author keeps reminding us of the differences between California and the Yukon—how does he do that?
- Why is it important that Madge, Walter, and Skiff Miller trust each other?

Brown Wolf

by Jack London
Illustrated by Joel Snyder
adapted for young readers

Madge Irvine put on her walking shoes and walked to the front door of the small mountain cottage. Her husband Walt was waiting for her outside, enjoying the warm California sun. Madge looked at the forest that surrounded the cottage, then turned to her husband.

"Where's Wolf?" she asked.

"He was here a moment ago," said Walt. "He was chasing a rabbit the last I saw of him."

"Wolf! Wolf! Here, Wolf!" she called, as they left the cottage and took the trail that led down through the forest to the county road.

Walt put the little finger of each hand between his lips and began to whistle loudly. Madge and Walt heard a crashing in the bushes and then, forty feet above them, on the edge of a cliff, a large animal appeared.

His body and coat and tail were like a huge timber wolf's, but his color showed that he was really a dog. No wolf was ever colored like him. He was brown, deep brown, red-brown, brown in every way. His back and shoulders were a warm brown, and his belly was a brownish yellow. His throat and paws were light brown, and his eyes were golden.

Wolf's front legs knocked a pebble loose, and he watched the fall of the pebble with pointed ears and sharp eyes until it struck at the Irvine's feet. Then he looked right at them and seemed to laugh.

"Come here, Wolf," Walt called out to him.

His ears flattened back and down at the sound as if an invisible hand was patting him on the head. They watched him scramble into the forest. Then they proceeded on their way. He joined them several minutes later, but he did not stay for long. A pat and a rub around the ears from the man, and a longer hug from the woman, and he was far down the trail in front of them, gliding effortlessly over the ground like a true wolf.

The man and woman loved the dog very much, but it had been hard for them to win his love. He had drifted in about three years ago. Tired and hungry, he had killed a rabbit right next to their cottage, and then crawled away and slept by the spring at the foot of the blackberry bushes. He had snarled at Walt the next morning, and he had snarled at Madge when she gave him a large pan of bread and milk.

Wolf continued to be an unfriendly dog, and refused to let them lay hands on him. Every time they came near, he would show his fangs and his hair would bristle. But he remained by the blackberry bushes, sleeping and resting, and eating the food they gave him. He remained because he was weak, and several days later, when he felt better, he disappeared.

And that should have been the end of him. But, the very next day, Walt had to take a business trip north, to Oregon. Riding along on the train, near the California-Oregon border, he happened to look out of the window and saw his unfriendly guest moving along the road, tired, dust-covered, and soiled from two hundred miles of travel.

Walt got off the train at the next station, bought a piece of meat, and captured the dog on the outskirts of the town. Walt transported Wolf back to Glen Ellen in the baggage car, and took him back to the mountain cottage. Wolf was tied up for a week, and the Irvines tried everything to make him happy. But he only snarled at their soft-spoken love words.

They soon discovered that he never barked. In all the time they had him, he never barked.

To win Wolf's affection became a problem. Walt liked problems. He had a metal tag made, on which was stamped: "Return to Walt Irvine, Glen Ellen, California." This tag was put on a collar and strapped around the dog's neck. Then Wolf was turned loose, and he promptly disappeared. A day later, a telegram came from a county over one hundred miles north. In twenty hours, the dog had gone over a hundred miles and was still going north when he was captured.

Wolf was sent back by train. The Irvines tied him up for three days, and he was let loose on the fourth, and he left once again. This time he got all the way north to Oregon when he was caught and returned. Always, as soon as he received his freedom, he fled—and always he fled north.

Another time, the dog crossed all of Oregon, and most of Washington, before he was picked up and returned. The speed with which he traveled was remarkable. On the first day's run he was known to cover as much as a hundred and fifty miles, and after that he would go a hundred miles a day until caught. He always arrived back lean and hungry and mean, and always left fresh and lively, making his way northward for some reason that no one could understand.

But at last, after a year of running away, he accepted the Irvines and decided to remain at the cottage where he had killed the rabbit and slept by the spring. After he decided to stay, a long time went by before he allowed the man and woman to pet him. He only liked the Irvines and no guest at the cottage could ever make friends with him. A low growl greeted every approach. If anyone was foolish enough to come nearer, the naked fangs appeared, and the growl became a snarl.

The Irvines could only guess at his past life. They figured that he must have come up from the south when he first came to their cottage. Mrs. Johnson, their nearest neighbor, thought he was a Yukon dog. She said that her brother, who was looking for gold up there, had told her about dogs like Wolf.

The Irvines agreed with Mrs. Johnson. The tips of Wolf's ears had obviously been so severely frozen at some time that they would never quite heal again. Besides, he looked like the photographs of the Yukon dogs they saw in magazines and newspapers. They often wondered about his past, and tried to imagine what his Yukon life had been like. They knew that the north still drew him, for at night they sometimes heard him crying softly; and when the north wind blew and the bite of frost was in the air, he would let out a sad cry like a long wolf howl. Yet he never barked; nothing could make him bark.

Part 2
* * *

Wolf paused by Madge and Walt for a quick pat on the head. Then he glided quickly ahead of them. Both Madge and Walt seemed to be thinking about Wolf as they followed him down the path. It was a long way to the county road, and when they came to a clearing, they sat down on a log.

A tiny stream flowed out of the forest, dropped over a slippery stone, and ran across the path at their feet. From the valley arose the song of meadowlarks, while around them great yellow butterflies fluttered in and out, through sunshine and shadow.

They heard a sound from the path. It was a crunching of heavy feet. As Walt and Madge looked at each other, a man came into view around the turn of the trail. He was sweaty. With a handkerchief in one hand he mopped his face, while in the other hand he carried a new hat. He was a well-built man, and his muscles seemed on the point of bursting out of the new black clothes he wore.

"Warm day," said Walt.

The man paused and nodded. "I guess I ain't much used to the warmth," he said. "I'm used to cold weather."

"You don't find any of that in this country," Walt laughed.

"Should say not," the man answered. "And I ain't lookin' for it either. I'm trying to find my sister. Maybe you know where she lives. Her name's Johnson, Mrs. William Johnson."

"You must be her Yukon brother!" Madge cried, her eyes bright with interest. "We've heard so much about you."

"Yes ma'am, that's me," he answered. "My name's Miller, Skiff Miller. I just thought I'd surprise her."

Madge stood up to show Skiff Miller the way to his sister's house. "Do you see that redwood?" she said, pointing up the canyon. "Take the little trail that turns off to the right. It's the shortcut to her house. You can't miss it."

"Yes'm, thank you, ma'am," he said.

"We'd like to hear you tell about the Yukon," Madge said. "Could we come over one day while you are at your sister's? Or, better yet, won't you come over and have dinner with us?"

"Yes'm, thank you, ma'am," he mumbled. Then he continued, "I ain't stopping long. I have to be pulling north again. I go out on tonight's train."

Madge was about to say that it was too bad, when Wolf trotted into the clearing.

Skiff Miller froze. He had eyes only for the dog, and a great wonder came into his face. "Well, I'll be hanged," he said, slowly and solemnly.

He sat down on the log, leaving Madge standing. At the sound of his voice, Wolf's ears had flattened down, then his mouth had opened in a laugh. He trotted slowly up to the stranger and first smelled his hands, then licked them.

Skiff Miller patted the dog's head and slowly and solemnly repeated, "Well, I'll be hanged."

"Excuse me, ma'am," he said the next moment. "I was just surprised, that's all."

"We're surprised, too," she answered slowly. "We never saw Wolf act friendly toward a stranger."

"Is that what you call him—Wolf?" Miller asked.

Madge nodded. "But I can't understand his friendliness toward you—unless it's because you're from the Yukon. He's a Yukon dog, you know."

"Yes'm," Miller said, working away. He lifted one of Wolf's forelegs and examined the footpads, pressing them and denting them with his thumb. "Kind of soft," he remarked. "He ain't been on a trail for a long time."

"I say," Walt broke in, "it's remarkable the way he lets you handle him."

Skiff Miller got up and asked, sharply, "How long have you had him?"

But just then the dog, squirming and rubbing against the newcomer's legs, opened his mouth and barked. It was a loud bark, brief and joyous, but a bark.

Walt and Madge stared at each other. The miracle had happened. Wolf had barked.

"It's the first time he ever barked," Madge said.

"First time I ever heard him, too," Miller replied.

Madge smiled at Miller. "Of course," she said, "since you have only seen him for five minutes."

Skiff Miller looked at her. "I thought you understood," he said slowly. "I thought you'd figured it out from the way he acted. He's my dog. His name ain't Wolf. It's Brown."

"Oh, Walt!" Madge cried to her husband.

Walt demanded, "How do you know he's your dog?"

"Because he is," was the reply.

"That's no proof," Walt said sharply.

In his slow way, Skiff Miller looked at the dog, then said, "The dog's mine. I raised him and I guess I ought to know. Look here. I'll prove it to you."

Skiff Miller turned to the dog. "Brown!" His voice rang out sharply, and at the sound the dog's ears flattened down. "Gee!" The dog made a swinging turn to the right. "Now mush on!" Abruptly the dog stopped turning and started straight ahead, halting obediently at command.

"I can do it with whistles," Skiff Miller said proudly. "He was my lead dog. Somebody stole him from me three years ago, and I've been looking for him ever since."

Madge's voice trembled as she asked, "But—but are you going to take him away with you?"

The man nodded.

Madge asked, "Back into that awful Yukon?"

He nodded and added, "Oh, it ain't so bad as all that. Look at me. Pretty healthy man—ain't I?"

"But the dogs! The terrible hardship, the heartbreaking work, the starvation, the frost! Oh, I've read about it and I know."

Miller said nothing.

Madge paused a moment, then said, "Why not leave him here? He is happy. He'll never suffer from hunger—you know that. He'll never suffer from cold and hardship. Everything is soft and gentle here. He will never feel a whip again. And as for the weather—why, it never snows here."

"Yes, it's hot here," Skiff Miller said and laughed.

"But answer me," Madge continued. "What do you have to offer him in that Yukon life?"

"Food, when I've got it, and that's most of the time," came the answer.

"And the rest of the time?"

"No food."

"And the work?"

"Yes, plenty of work," Miller blurted out impatiently. "Work without end, and hunger, and frost, and all the rest of the hardships—that's what he'll get when he comes with me. But he likes it. He's used to it. He knows that life. He was born to it and brought up in it. And you don't know anything about it—you don't know what you're talking about. That's where the dog belongs, and that's where he'll be happiest."

"The dog doesn't go," Walt announced "So there is no need for any more talk."

"What's that?" Skiff Miller demanded. His brows lowered and his face became flushed.

"I said, the dog doesn't go, and that settles it," Walt said. "I don't believe he's your dog. You may have seen him sometime. You may have sometimes driven him for his owner. But his obeying the ordinary driving commands of the trail doesn't prove that he is yours. Any dog in the Yukon would obey you as he obeyed. Besides, he is probably a valuable dog, and that might explain why you want to have him."

Skiff Miller's huge muscles bulged under the black cloth of his black coat as he carefully looked Walt up and down. His face hardened, then he said, "I reckon there's nothing in sight to prevent me from taking the dog right here and now."

Walt's face flushed, and the striking muscles of his arms and shoulders seemed to stiffen and grow tense. Madge quickly stepped between the two men.

"Maybe Mr. Miller is right," she said. "I am afraid that he is. Wolf does seem to know him, and certainly he answers to the name of 'Brown.' He made friends with him instantly, and you know that's something he never did with anybody before. Besides, look at the way he barked. He was just bursting with joy."

"Joy over what?" asked Walt.

"Finding Mr. Miller, I think," answered Madge.

Walt's striking muscles relaxed, and his shoulders seemed to droop with hopelessness. "I guess you're right, Madge," he said. "Wolf isn't Wolf, but Brown. He must belong to Mr. Miller."

Part 3
***

The three people were silent for a moment, then Madge brightened up and said, "Perhaps Mr. Miller will sell us the dog. We can buy him."

Skiff Miller shook his head. "I had five dogs," he said. "Wolf was the leader. Somebody once offered me twelve hundred dollars for him. I didn't sell him then, and I ain't selling him now. Besides, I think a mighty lot of that dog. I've been looking for him for three years. I couldn't believe my eyes when I saw him just now. I thought I was dreaming. It was too good to be true."

"But the dog," Madge said quickly. "You haven't considered the dog."

Skiff Miller looked puzzled.

"Have you thought about him?" she asked.

"I don't know what you're driving at," Miller said.

"Maybe the dog has some choice in the matter," Madge went on. "Maybe he has his likes and dislikes. You haven't considered him. You give him no choice. It hasn't even entered your mind that he might prefer California to Alaska. You consider only what you like. You treat him like a sack of potatoes."

This was a new way of looking at it, and Miller's face hardened as he started to think to himself.

"If you really love him," Madge continued, "you would want him to be happy, no matter where he is."

Miller asked, "Do you think he'd sooner stay in California?"

Madge nodded her head. "I'm sure of it."

Skiff Miller started thinking out loud. "He was a good worker. He's done a lot of work for me. He never loafed on me, and he was great at getting a new team into shape. He's got a head on him. He can do everything but talk. He knows we're talking about him."

The dog was lying at Skiff Miller's feet, his head down close to his paws, his ears erect and listening. His eyes were quick and eager to follow the sounds of one person and then the other.

Miller went on. "There's a lot of work in him yet. He'll be good for years to come."

Skiff Miller opened his mouth and closed it again without speaking. Finally he said, "I'll tell you what I'll do. Your remarks, ma'am, make sense. He has worked hard, and maybe he's earned a soft place and has got a right to choose. Anyway, we'll leave it up to him. Whatever he says, goes. You people stay right here sitting down. I'll say goodbye, and I'll walk off. If he wants to stay, he can stay. If he wants to come with me, let him come. I won't call him to come and don't you call him to come back."

Miller paused a moment, then added, "Only, you must play fair. Don't call him after my back is turned."

"We'll play fair," Madge said. "I don't know how to thank you."

"I don't see that you've got any reason to thank me," he replied. "Brown ain't decided yet. Now you won't mind if I go away slow? It's only fair, since I'll be out of sight in a hundred yards."

Madge agreed, and added, "and I promise you that we won't do anything to try to change his mind."

"Well, then, I might as well be getting along," Skiff Miller said. And he got ready to leave.

Wolf lifted his head quickly, and still more quickly got to his feet when Miller shook hands with Madge. Wolf sprang up on his hind legs, resting his forepaws on Madge's hip and at the same time, licking Skiff Miller's hand. When Miller shook hands with Walt, Wolf repeated his act, resting his weight on Walt and licking both men's hands.

"It ain't no picnic, I can tell you that," Miller said. These were his last words, as he turned and went slowly up the trail.

Wolf watched him go about twenty feet, as though waiting for the man to turn and come back. Then, with a quick, low whine, Wolf sprang after him, caught up to him, gently grabbed Miller's hand between his teeth, and tried gently to make him stop.

But Miller did not stop. Wolf raced back to where Walt Irvine sat, catching his coat sleeve in his teeth and trying to drag him toward Miller.

Wolf wanted to be in two places at the same time, with the old master and the new, but the distance between them was increasing. He sprang about excitedly, making short nervous leaps and twists, now toward one person, now toward the other, not knowing his own mind, wanting both and unable to choose, uttering quick, sharp whines and beginning to pant.

He sat down, thrust his nose upward, and opened his mouth wide. He was ready to howl.

But just as the howl was about to burst from his throat, he closed his mouth and looked long and steadily at Miller's back. Suddenly Wolf turned his head, and looked just as steadily at Walt. The dog received no sign, no suggestion and no clue as to what he should do.

As Wolf glanced ahead to where the old master was nearing the curve of the trail, Wolf became excited again. He sprang to his feet with a whine, and then, struck by a new idea, turned toward Madge. He had ignored her up to now, but now, he went over to her and snuggled his head in her lap, nudging her arm with his nose— an old trick of his when begging for favors. He backed away from her and began to twist playfully. All his body, from his twinkling eyes and flattened ears to the wagging tail, begged her to tell him what to do. But Madge did not move.

The dog stopped playing. He was saddened by the coldness of these people who had never been cold before.

He turned and gently gazed after the old master. Skiff Miller was rounding the curve. In a moment he would be gone from view. Yet he never turned his head, plodding straight onward, as though he had no interest in what was occurring behind his back.

And then he went out of view. Wolf waited for him to reappear. He waited a long minute, silently, without movement, as though turned to stone. He barked once, and waited. Then he turned and trotted back to Walt Irvine. He sniffed his hand and dropped down heavily at his feet, watching the trail where it curved from view.

The tiny stream that slipped down the stone seemed to gurgle more loudly than before. Except for the meadowlarks, there was no other sound. The great yellow butterflies drifted silently through the sunshine and lost themselves in the sleepy shadows. Madge smiled at her husband.

A few minutes later Wolf got on his feet. His movements were decisive. He did not glance at the man and woman. His eyes were fixed on the trail. He had made up his mind. They knew it. And they knew that they had lost.

Wolf started to trot away, and Madge had to force herself not to call him back. She remembered the promise she had made to Skiff Miller. Walt's solemn look showed that he also remembered the promise.

Wolf's trot broke into a run. He made leaps that were longer and longer. Not once did he turn his head. He cut sharply across the curve of the trail and was gone.

Extending Comprehension

Story Questions

1. Is Wolf one of the main characters in the story? Tell why or why not.
2. Describe at least three of the many things Madge and Walt did to win Wolf's love.
3. What do we learn about Wolf that makes people think he is from the north?
4. Compare how Wolf treats Skiff Miller to how he treats other strangers.
5. Why does Madge think Wolf will be happier in California?
6. Why was it so necessary for Madge, Walter, and Skiff Miller to trust each other?
7. Why do you think Wolf decided to go with Skiff Miller?
8. Why is "Brown Wolf" a good title for the story?

Discussion Topics

1. Wolf has to choose between the easy life in California and the hard life in the Yukon. Discuss the advantages of living in each place. During your discussion, think about the answers to the following questions:
   - What kind of life did Wolf have in California? What was the weather like? When did he eat? Did he work?
   - What kind of life did he have in the Yukon? What was the weather like? When did he eat? What kind of work did he do?
2. Wolf treated Skiff Miller differently than he treated other strangers. He also responded to Skiff Miller's commands. Discuss the different responses Wolf made to Skiff Miller. During your discussion, attempt to answer the following questions:
   - How did Wolf first respond? How did he respond to Skiff Miller after that?
   - At what point in the story were you convinced that the dog belonged to Skiff?
   - Would a California dog know to respond to the commands "gee" and "now mush on"? Explain your answer.
3. Discuss the events at the end of the story that let you know how undecided Wolf was. During your discussion, try to answer the following questions:
   - What things did Wolf do that let you know he was struggling to make up his mind?
   - Where do you think Wolf should have gone?

Writing Ideas

1. The author doesn't tell you some important things about this story. He doesn't tell you how Wolf got from the Yukon to California. He only tells you that he was stolen from Skiff Miller. Write down your idea of what happened. Tell who stole Brown, how that person and Brown got to California, and how Brown got away from that person.
2. You have read two stories by Jack London. Strong dogs that are very loyal to their owners are important characters in these two stories. Write your own story about a strong and loyal dog. It can be about a dog you know or about a dog you wish you knew.
3. Madge, Walt, and Skiff Miller had to trust each other to not call out to Wolf. Did they keep their trust? Write about a time in your life that it was particularly important for you to be trusted and what would have happened if you hadn't kept your trust.

STORY 6
AFTER LESSON 60

Like Jake and Me

by Mavis Jukes
Illustrated by James Watling

New Vocabulary Words

1. Stetson hat
2. raven
3. nectar
4. steer
5. entomologist
6. landscape
7. cautiously
8. grapple
9. swagger

Definitions

1. A **Stetson hat** is a particular brand of hat that always looks the same. A Stetson is made out of felt, has a wide brim and a high crown. Cowboys often wear Stetsons.
2. A **raven** is a large black bird that makes a loud, unpleasant noise.
3. **Nectar** is the juice from a fruit.
4. A **steer** is a male cow that is raised for beef.
5. An **entomologist** is a scientist who studies insects.
6. Another word for *scenery* is **landscape.**
7. When you do something **cautiously,** you do it with caution and care.
8. When you **grapple** with something, you struggle with that thing.
9. When you **swagger,** you walk like you think you are very important.

Story Background

The author of "Like Jake and Me," Mavis Jukes, lives in northern California. Her house is in the country. She is a lawyer, but she writes books for young people. She likes to write **realistic fiction**—stories about regular people involved in everyday situations. Her story, "Like Jake and Me," is a good example of this kind of fiction.

"Like Jake and Me" is about a young boy, Alex, his mother, and his stepfather. These characters may remind you of people you know. Although the story is about a serious topic, the relationship between Alex and his stepfather is very funny as well.

Mavis Jukes also writes realistically about the setting of the story. Most of "Like Jake and Me" takes place outdoors in a setting with lots of trees. We can imagine how those trees look if we know something about them. The story begins near a cypress grove, which is a small woods of cypress trees. Cypress trees are evergreens, which means that their leaves are green all year long. Later in the story, you will read about poplar trees growing on the distant hills. Poplar trees are tall and narrow. They lose their leaves in the winter. The story takes place in the fall, so the leaves of poplar trees are yellow. We know the leaves will soon fall off these trees. You will also read about a pear tree that has pears growing in an unusual way.

Focus Questions

- Why does Alex think he is so different from Jake?
- Why does Jake think he is so different from Alex?
- Why do you think the story is titled "Like Jake and Me"?

Like Jake and Me

by Mavis Jukes
Illustrated by James Watling

The rain had stopped. The sun was setting. There were clouds in the sky the color of smoke. Alex was watching his stepfather, Jake, split wood at the edge of the cypress grove. Somewhere a toad was grunting.

"Jake!" called Alex.

Jake swung the axe, and wood flew into the air.

"Jake!" Alex called again. "Need me?" Alex had a loose tooth in front. He moved it in and out with his tongue.

Jake rested the axe head in the grass and leaned on the handle. "What?" he said. He took off his Stetson hat and wiped his forehead on his jacket sleeve.

Alex cupped his hands around his mouth. "Do . . . you . . . need . . . me . . . to . . . help?" he hollered. Then he tripped over a pumpkin, fell on it, and broke it. A toad flopped away.

Jake adjusted the raven feather behind his hatband. "Better stay there!" he called. He put his hat back on. With powerful arms, he sunk the axe blade into a log. It fell in half.

"Wow," thought Alex. "I'll never be able to do that."

Alex's mother was standing close by, under the pear tree. She was wearing fuzzy woolen leg warmers, a huge knitted coat with pictures of reindeer on the back, and a red scarf with the name *Virginia* on it. "I need you," she said.

Alex stood up, dumped the pumpkin over the fence for the sheep, and went to Virginia.

"I dropped two quarters and a dime in the grass. If I bend down, I may never be able to get up again," she said. Virginia was enormous. She was pregnant with twins, and her belly blocked her view to the ground. "I can't even see where they fell."

"Here!" said Alex. He gave her two quarters. Then he found the dime. He tied her shoe while he was down there.

"Thanks," said Virginia. "I also need you for some advice." She pointed up. "Think it's ready?"

One of the branches of the pear tree had a glass bottle over the end of it. Inside were some twigs and leaves and two pears. In the spring, Virginia had pushed the bottle onto the branch, over the blossoms. During the summer, the pears had grown and sweetened inside the bottle. Now they were fat and crowding each other.

The plan was that when the pears were ripe, Virginia would pull the bottle from the tree, leaving the fruit inside. Then she'd fill the bottle with pear nectar and trick her sister, Caroline. Caroline would never guess how Virginia got the pears into the bottle!

"Shall we pick it?" asked Virginia.

"Up to you!" said Alex.

Months ago, Virginia had told him that the pears, and the babies, would be ready in the fall. Alex looked away at the hills. They were dusky gray. There were smudges of yellow poplars on the land. Autumn was here.

Alex fiddled with his tooth. "Mom," he asked, "do you think the twins are brothers or sisters?"

"Maybe both," said Virginia.

"If there's a boy, do you think he'll be like Jake or like me?"

"Maybe like Jake and you," said Virginia.

"Like Jake and me?" Alex wondered how that could be possible.

"Right," said Virginia.

"Well, anyway," said Alex, "would you like to see something I can do?"

"Of course," she said.

Alex straightened. Gracefully he lifted his arms and rose up on his toes. He looked like a bird about to take off. Then he lowered his arms and crouched. Suddenly he sprang up. He spun once around in midair and landed lightly.

Virginia clapped. "Great!"

Alex did it again, faster. Then again, and again. He whirled and danced around the tree for Virginia. He spun until he was pooped. Jake had put down the axe and was watching.

"Ballet class!" gasped Alex. "Dad signed me up for lessons, remember?"

"Of course I remember," said Virginia. "Go show Jake!"

"No," panted Alex. "Jake isn't the ballet type."

"He might like it," said Virginia. "Go see!"

"Maybe another time," said Alex. He raced across the field to where Jake was loading his arms with logs. "Jake, I'll carry the axe."

"Carry the axe?" Jake shook his head. "I just sharpened that axe."

Alex moved his tooth with his tongue and squinted up at Jake. "I'm careful," he said.

Jake looked over at the sheep nosing the pumpkin. "Maybe another time," he told Alex.

Alex walked beside him as they headed toward the house. The air was so cold Jake was breathing steam. The logs were stacked to his chin.

Virginia stood under the pear tree, watching the sunset. Alex ran past her to open the door.

Jake thundered up the stairs and onto the porch. His boots were covered with moss and dirt. Alex stood in the doorway.

"Watch it!" said Jake. He shoved the door open farther with his shoulder, and Alex backed up against the wall. Jake moved sideways through the door.

"Here, I'll help you stack the wood!" said Alex.

"Watch it!" Jake came down on one knee and set the wood by the side of the woodstove. Then he said kindly, "You've really got to watch it, Alex. I can't see where I'm going with so big a load."

Alex wiggled his tooth with his tongue. "I just wanted to help you," he said. He went to Jake and put his hand on Jake's shoulder. Then he leaned around and looked under his Stetson hat. There was bark in Jake's beard. "You look like a cowboy in the movies."

"I have news for you," said Jake. "I *am* a cowboy. A real one." He unsnapped his jacket. On his belt buckle was a silver longhorn steer. "Or was one." He looked over at Alex.

Alex shoved his tooth forward with his tongue.

"Why don't you just pull out that tooth?" Jake asked him.

"Too chicken," said Alex. He closed his mouth.

"Well, everybody's chicken of something," said Jake. He opened his jacket pocket and took out a wooden match. He chewed on the end of it and looked out the windows behind the stove. He could see Virginia, still standing beneath the tree. Her hands were folded under her belly.

Jake balled up newspaper and broke some sticks. He had giant hands. He filled the woodstove with the wadded paper and the sticks and pushed in a couple of logs.

"Can I light the fire?" Alex asked.

"Maybe another time," said Jake. He struck the match on his rodeo belt buckle. He lit the paper and threw the match into the fire.

Just then Alex noticed that there was a wolf spider on the back of Jake's neck. There were fuzzy babies holding on to her body. "Did you know wolf spiders carry their babies around?" said Alex.

"Says who?" asked Jake.

"My dad," said Alex. He moved his tooth out as far as it would go. "He's an entomologist, remember?"

"I remember," said Jake.

"Dad says they only bite you if you bother them, or if you're squashing them," said Alex. "But still, I never mess with wolf spiders." He pulled his tooth back in with his tongue.

"Is that what he says, huh," said Jake. He jammed another log into the stove, then looked out again at Virginia. She was gazing at the landscape. The hills were fading. The farms were fading. The cypress trees were turning black.

"I think she's pretty," said Alex, looking at the spider.

"I do, too," said Jake, looking at Virginia.

"It's a nice design on her back," said Alex, examining the spider.

"Yep!" said Jake. He admired the reindeer coat, which he'd loaned to Virginia.

"Her belly sure is big!" said Alex.

"It has to be, to carry the babies," said Jake.

"She's got an awful lot of babies there," said Alex.

Jake laughed. Virginia was shaped something like a pear.

"And boy! Are her legs woolly!" said Alex.

Jake looked at Virginia's leg warmers. "Itchy," said Jake. He rubbed his neck. The spider crawled over his collar.

"She's in your coat!" said Alex. He backed away a step.

"We can share it," said Jake. He liked to see Virginia bundled up. "It's big enough for both of us. She's got to stay warm." Jake stood up.

"You sure are brave," Alex said. "I like wolf spiders, but I wouldn't have let that one into my coat. That's the biggest, hairiest wolf spider I've ever seen."

Jake froze. "Wolf spider! Where?"

"In your coat getting warm," said Alex.

Jake stared at Alex. "What wolf spider?"

"The one we were talking about, with the babies!" said Alex. "And the furry legs."

"Wolf spider!" Jake moaned. "I thought we were talking about Virginia!" He was holding his shoulders up around his ears.

"You never told me you were scared of spiders," said Alex.

"You never asked me," said Jake in a high voice. "Help!"

"How?" asked Alex.

"Get my jacket off!"

Alex took hold of Jake's jacket sleeve as Jake eased his arm out. Cautiously, Alex took the jacket from Jake's shoulders. Alex looked in the coat.

"No spider, Jake," said Alex. "I think she went into your shirt."

"My shirt?" asked Jake. "You think?"

"Maybe," said Alex.

Jake gasped. "Inside? I hope not!"

"Feel anything furry crawling on you?" asked Alex.

"Anything *furry* crawling on me?" Jake shuddered. "No!"

"Try to get your shirt off without squashing her," said Alex. "Remember, we don't want to hurt her. She's a mama."

"With babies," added Jake. *"Eek!"*

"And," said Alex, "she'll bite!"

"Bite? Yes, I know!" said Jake. "Come out on the porch and help me! I don't want her to get loose in the house!"

Jake walked stiffly to the door. Alex opened it. They walked out onto the porch. The sky was thick gray and salmon colored, with blue windows through the clouds.

"Feel anything?" asked Alex.

"Something . . ." said Jake. He unsnapped the snaps on his sleeves, then the ones down the front. He opened his shirt. On his chest was a tattoo of an eagle that was either taking off or landing. He let the shirt drop to the floor.

"No spider, back or front," reported Alex.

They shook out the shirt.

"Maybe your jeans," said Alex. "Maybe she got into your jeans!"

"Not my *jeans!*" said Jake. He quickly undid his rodeo belt.

"Your boots!" said Alex. "First you have to take off your boots!"

"Right!" said Jake. He sat down on the boards. Each boot had a yellow rose and the name *Jake* stitched on the side. "Could you help?" he asked.

"Okay," said Alex. He grappled with one boot and got it off. He checked it. He pulled off and checked the sock. No spider. He tugged on the other boot.

"You've got to pull harder," said Jake, as Alex pulled and struggled. "Harder!"

The boot came off and smacked Alex in the mouth. "Ouch!" Alex put his tongue in the gap. "Knocked my tooth out!" He looked in the boot. "It's in the boot!"

"Yikes!" said Jake.

"Not the spider," said Alex. "My tooth." He rolled it out of the boot and into his hand to examine it.

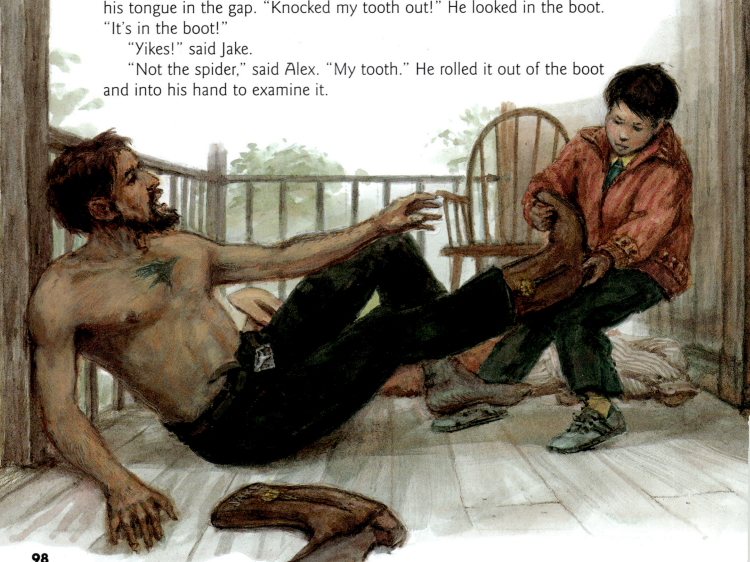

"Dang," said Jake. "Then hurry up." Alex dropped the tooth back into the boot. Jake climbed out of his jeans and looked down each leg. He hopped on one foot to get the other sock off.

"She won't be in your sock," said Alex. "But maybe—"

"Don't tell me," said Jake. "Not my shorts!"

Alex stared at Jake's shorts. There were pictures of mallard ducks on them. "Your shorts," said Alex.

"I'm afraid to look," said Jake. He thought he felt something creeping just below his belly button.

"Someone's coming!" said Alex. "Quick! Give me your hat! I'll hold it up and you can stand behind it."

"Help!" said Jake in a small voice. He gave Alex the hat and quickly stepped out of his shorts. He brushed himself off in the front.

"Okay in the back," said Alex, peering over the brim of the hat.

Jake turned his shorts inside out, then right side in again. No spider. When he bent over to put them on, he backed into his hat, and the raven feather poked him. Jake howled and jumped up and spun around in midair.

"I didn't know you could do ballet!" said Alex. "You dance like me!"

"I thought I felt the spider!" said Jake. He put on his shorts.

"What on *earth* are you doing?" huffed Virginia. She was standing at the top of the stairs, holding the bottle with the pears inside.

"We're hunting for a spider," said Jake.

"Well!" said Virginia. "I like your hunting outfit. But aren't those *duck*-hunting shorts, and aren't you cold?"

"We're not hunting spiders," explained Jake. "We're hunting *for* a spider."

"A big and hairy one that *bites!* " added Alex.

"A wolf spider!" said Jake, shivering. He had goose bumps.

"Really!" said Virginia. She set the bottle down beside Jake's boot. "Aha!" she cried, spying Alex's tooth inside. "Here's one of the spider's teeth!"

Alex grinned at this mother. He put his tongue where his tooth wasn't.

Jake took his hat from Alex and put it on.

"Hey!" said Virginia.

"What?" said Jake.

"The spider!" she said. "It's on your hat!"

"Help!" said Jake. "Somebody help me!"

Alex sprang up into the air and snatched the hat from Jake's head.

"Look!" said Alex.

"Holy smoke!" said Jake.

There, hiding behind the black feather, was the spider.

Alex tapped the hat brim. The spider dropped to the floor. Then off she swaggered with her fuzzy babies, across the porch and into a crack.

Jake went over to Alex. He knelt down. "Thanks, Alex," said Jake. It was the closest Alex had ever been to the eagle. Jake pressed Alex against its wings. "May I have this dance?" Jake asked.

Ravens were lifting from the blackening fields and calling. The last light had settled in the clouds like pink dust.

Jake stood up holding Alex, and together they looked at Virginia. She was rubbing her belly. "Something is happening here," she told them. "It feels like the twins are beginning to dance."

"Like Jake and me," said Alex. And Jake whirled around the porch with Alex in his arms.

Extending Comprehension

Story Questions

1. In the beginning of the story, what would Jake say when Alex offered to help him do something?
2. Why did Alex think he was so different from Jake?
3. Jake and Alex each had something they were afraid of. What were those things?
4. After Jake lit the fire, some funny things happened. Name at least three things that were funny.
5. Why do you think the story is titled "Like Jake and Me"?

Discussion Topics

1. Alex and Jake have a very funny conversation. Discuss what made this conversation so funny. During your discussion, try to answer the following questions:
   - Why did Jake and Alex think they were talking about the same topic?
   - The author uses imagery during this part of the story. This means the author's words helped you picture what was happening. Describe the picture you imagined during this funny part of the story.

2. Even though this story has a very funny part, it also has a serious message. The title of the story gives you a clue about its message. Talk about why this story is called "Like Jake and Me." During your discussion, try to answer the following questions:
   - At the beginning of the story, Alex and Jake thought they were very different from each other. In what way did they think they were different?
   - The experience with the spider helped Alex and Jake realize they were alike in some ways. How were they alike?

Writing Ideas

1. Pretend you are Virginia. Describe what you see when you get to your porch after Jake and Alex still haven't found the wolf spider. Be sure to tell what Jake looks like, what Alex is missing, and what things are on the porch. Tell what your reaction is when you see this situation.

2. Both Jake and Alex are afraid of certain things. Tell about something that frightens you. Tell why it frightens you and what you have tried to do so you aren't as afraid of it.

STORY 7
AFTER LESSON 70

Thank You, M'am

by Langston Hughes
Illustrated by Donald Cook

New Vocabulary Words

1. cocoa
2. contact
3. frail
4. kitchenette
5. latching
6. mistrusted
7. presentable
8. roomers
9. suede

Definitions

1. **Cocoa** is a hot drink made with milk and chocolate.
2. When things are in **contact,** they touch each other.
3. Something that is very weak or delicate is **frail**.
4. A **kitchenette** is a very small kitchen.
5. When you are **latching** onto something, you are grabbing it and hanging onto it.
6. **Mistrusted** means not trusted.
7. A person who is neat and clean is **presentable.**
8. **Roomers** are people who live in a rented room in a house.
9. **Suede** is leather that has a soft surface.

Story Background

"Thank You, M'am" is another example of realistic fiction. It was written by a famous African American author from Missouri named Langston Hughes. When he was 22 years old, Langston Hughes moved to Harlem in New York City. Harlem was and still is a neighborhood where black writers, musicians, and artists live and work. During the 1920s and 1930s in Harlem, Langston Hughes was one of the leaders in a group of creative people who celebrated their black traditions through writing and music. People refer to the work of this group as the Harlem Renaissance.

Langston Hughes is well known for his short stories, novels, plays, and poetry about the everyday experiences of black people. Even though the short story you will read was written in 1958, its message still rings true today.

103

Focus Questions

- What unexpected things does Mrs. Jones do for Roger?
- What do the two main characters have in common?
- What do you think Roger learns from Mrs. Jones?
- Why do you think the story is called "Thank You, M'am"?

Thank You, M'am

by Langston Hughes
Illustrated by Donald Cook

She was a large woman with a large purse that had everything in it but a hammer and nails. It had a long strap, and she carried it slung across her shoulder. It was about eleven o'clock at night, dark, and she was walking alone, when a boy ran up behind her and tried to snatch her purse. The strap broke with the sudden single tug the boy gave it from behind. But the boy's weight and the weight of the purse combined caused him to lose his balance. Instead of taking off full blast as he had hoped, the boy fell on his back on the sidewalk, and his legs flew up. The large woman simply turned around and kicked him right square in his blue-jeaned sitter. Then she reached down, picked the boy up by his shirt front, and shook him until his teeth rattled.

After that the woman said, "Pick up my pocketbook, boy, and give it here."

She still held him tightly. But she bent down enough to permit him to stoop and pick up her purse. Then she said, "Now ain't you ashamed of yourself?"

Firmly gripped by his shirt front, the boy said, "Yes'm."

The woman said, "What did you want to do it for?"

The boy said, "I didn't aim to."

She said, "You a lie!"

By that time two or three people passed, stopped, turned to look, and some stood watching.

"If I turn you loose, will you run?" asked the woman.

"Yes'm," said the boy.

"Then I won't turn you loose," said the woman. She did not release him.

"Lady, I'm sorry," whispered the boy.

"Um-hum! Your face is dirty. I got a great mind to wash your face for you. Ain't you got nobody home to tell you to wash your face?"

"No'm," said the boy.

"Then it will get washed this evening," said the large woman, starting up the street, dragging the frightened boy behind her.

He looked as if he were fourteen or fifteen, frail and willow-wild, in tennis shoes and blue jeans.

The woman said, "You ought to be my son. I would teach you right from wrong. Least I can do right now is to wash your face. Are you hungry?"

"No'm," said the being-dragged boy. "I just want you to turn me loose."

"Was I bothering *you* when I turned that corner?" asked the woman.

"No'm."

"But you put yourself in contact with *me*," said the woman. "If you think that that contact is not going to last a while, you got another thing coming. When I get through with you, sir, you are going to remember Mrs. Luella Bates Washington Jones."

Sweat popped out on the boy's face, and he began to struggle. Mrs. Jones stopped, jerked him around in front of her, put a half nelson around his neck, and continued to drag him up the street. When she got to her door, she dragged the boy inside, down a hall, and into a large kitchenette-furnished room at the rear of the house. She switched on the light and left the door open. The boy could hear other roomers laughing and talking in the large house. Some of their doors were open, too, so he knew he and the woman were not alone. The woman still had him by the neck in the middle of her room.

She said, "What is your name?"

"Roger," answered the boy.

"Then, Roger, you go to that sink and wash your face," said the woman, whereupon she turned him loose—at last. Roger looked at the door—looked at the woman—looked at the door—and went to the sink.

"Let the water run until it gets warm," she said. "Here's a clean towel."

"You gonna take me to jail?" asked the boy, bending over the sink.

"Not with that face, I would not take you nowhere," said the woman. "Here I am trying to get home to cook me a bite to eat, and you snatch my pocketbook! Maybe you ain't been to your supper either, late as it be. Have you?"

"There's nobody home at my house," said the boy.

"Then we'll eat," said the woman. "I believe you're hungry—or been hungry—to try to snatch my pocketbook!"

"I want a pair of blue suede shoes," said the boy.

"Well, you didn't have to snatch my pocketbook to get some suede shoes," said Mrs. Luella Bates Washington Jones. "You could have asked me."

"M'am?"

The water dripping from his face, the boy looked at her. There was a long pause. A very long pause. After he had dried his face, and not knowing what else to do, dried it again, the boy turned around, wondering what next. The door was open. He could make a dash for it down the hall. He could run, run, run, *run!*

The woman was sitting on the daybed. After a while she said, "I were young once, and I wanted things I could not get."

There was another long pause. The boy's mouth opened. Then he frowned, not knowing he frowned.

The woman said, "Um-hum! You thought I was going to say *but,* didn't you? You thought I was going to say *but I didn't snatch people's pocketbooks.* Well, I wasn't going to say that." Pause. Silence. "I have done things, too, which I would not tell you, son—neither tell God, if He didn't already know. Everybody's got something in common. So you set down while I fix us something to eat. You might run that comb through your hair so you will look presentable."

In another corner of the room behind a screen was a gas plate and an icebox. Mrs. Jones got up and went behind the screen. The woman did not watch the boy to see if he was going to run now, nor did she watch her purse, which she left behind on the daybed. But the boy took care to sit on the far side of the room, away from the purse, where he thought she could easily see him out of the corner of her eye if she wanted to. He did not trust the woman *not* to trust him. And he did not want to be mistrusted now.

"Do you need somebody to go to the store," asked the boy, "maybe to get some milk or something?"

"Don't believe I do," said the woman, "unless you just want sweet milk yourself. I was going to make cocoa out of this canned milk I got here."

"That will be fine," said the boy.

She heated some lima beans and ham she had in the icebox, made the cocoa, and set the table. The woman did not ask the boy anything about where he lived, or his folks, or anything else that would embarrass him. Instead, as they ate, she told him about her job in a hotel beauty shop that stayed open late, what the work was like, and how all kinds of women came in and out, blondes, redheads, and Spanish. Then she cut him a half of her ten-cent cake.

"Eat some more, son," she said.

When they were finished eating, she got up and said, "Now here, take this ten dollars and buy yourself some blue suede shoes. And next time, do not make the mistake of latching onto *my* pocketbook *nor anybody else's*—because shoes got by devilish ways will burn your feet. I got to get my rest now. But from here on in, son, I hope you will behave yourself."

She led him down the hall to the front door and opened it. "Good night! Behave yourself, boy!" she said, looking out into the street as he went down the steps.

The boy wanted to say something other than, "Thank you, m'am," to Mrs. Luella Bates Washington Jones, but although his lips moved, he couldn't even say that as he turned at the foot of the barren stoop and looked up at the large woman in the door. Then she shut the door.

Extending Comprehension

Story Questions

1. What unexpected things did Mrs. Jones do for Roger?
2. Why do you think Roger decided against running away, even though he had the chance?
3. What did the two main characters have in common?
4. What do you think Roger learned from Mrs. Jones?
5. Why do you think the story is titled "Thank You, M'am"?

Discussion Topics

1. This story is titled "Thank You, M'am" but these words were never said in the story. During your discussion, try to answer the following questions:
   - Why do you think Roger couldn't say the words "Thank you, M'am" at the end of the story?
   - Why do you think the author chose that title but never had a character speak those words?

2. Mrs. Jones treated Roger differently than you might have expected, considering that he tried to steal her pocketbook. What would you have done to Roger if you were Mrs. Jones? During your discussion, try to answer the following questions:
   - What would you have said to Roger?
   - Would you have called the police? Explain your answer.

Writing Ideas

1. You've probably heard the expression, "you can't judge a book by its cover." Explain what this means and tell how it relates to Roger's experience with Mrs. Jones.

2. Pretend you are Roger. You are now grown up and have a teenage son of your own. Write a conversation between your son and you that explains how that day with Mrs. Jones changed your life. Be sure to include questions your son would ask you.

The Circuit

by Francisco Jiménez
Illustrated by Meryl Henderson

New Vocabulary Words

1. sharecropper
2. pickers
3. shack
4. jalopy
5. vineyard
6. savor
7. cities in California:
   - Fresno
   - Santa Maria
   - Santa Rosa

Definitions

1. A **sharecropper** is someone who rents land from a farmer.
2. People who harvest fruits and vegetables are sometimes called **pickers.**
3. A house that needs lots of fixing up is a **shack.**
4. Another way of saying *an old car that needs a lot of fixing up* is **jalopy.**
5. A **vineyard** is a field where grapevines grow.
6. **Savor** is another word for *appreciate.*
7. **Cities in California: Fresno, Santa Maria,** and **Santa Rosa.**

Story Background

The author of "The Circuit," Francisco Jiménez, wrote the story to tell about the lives of California farm workers. The narrator is a young boy. As you read the story, you will learn about the narrator's family and the work that he, his brother, and his father do. You will also learn about the food his mother cooks for the family and the places they live.

Even though the story takes place in California during the 1950s, it is a story that could be told about many places today. Like many farm workers who come to work in the United States, the narrator's family is from Mexico. California farmers need extra workers to help them with planting and harvesting their crops. Like many farm workers today, the narrator's family stays in one place and then, when the crops have been harvested in that place, they move to another place. Sometimes families stay in as many as six different places in one year. They live in labor camps, old houses, and sometimes, like the family of the narrator, garages.

During the harvest season, farm workers work for many long hours every day. Sometimes they work seven days a week. The crops must be harvested when they are ready. The work is very hard, and usually the sun is very hot. Children often work alongside their parents. In the story, the oldest children work in the fields with their father instead of going to school.

The story opens near the end of the strawberry harvest. Ito, a Japanese sharecropper, is in charge of the workers. Ito is unhappy because the best part of the strawberry season is over. Read the story to see what happens to some of the workers.

Many people have worked over the years to improve the working and living conditions of the farm workers who come to work in California and other states.

The family in the story speaks Spanish. The author uses some Spanish words to make his story seem more real. The Spanish words are in italics. The author gives the translation for some of these words in parentheses. For example, he writes *es todo* (that's it) and *mi olla* (my pot). Other times you will see Spanish words in italics without a translation. You can sometimes figure out the meaning of these words from the other words in the sentence.

Here are some words to try to figure out. The sentences that the words are in may help you. If you already speak Spanish, this will be easy for you!

- The *braceros* came from Mexico to work on the big farms of California.
- He came from *Jalisco* in Mexico. She came from Arizona in the United States.
- When the bell rang, the teacher said, "*Ya esora*. Get your things together and line up."
- I like to listen to Mexican *corridos* as much as I like to listen to rap. *Corrido* singers tell true stories about people or horses or ranches.
- When the game was over, my brother said, "*Vámonos*," and we walked home.

Focus Questions

- What kind of work do the father and his sons do?
- Where do they work, and how long do they work each day?
- What kinds of places does the family live in?
- Why does the family have to move from one place to another?
- How does the narrator feel about moving?
- Why does the narrator like school?
- What do packed cardboard boxes mean to the narrator?
- Why does the story have the title, "The Circuit"?

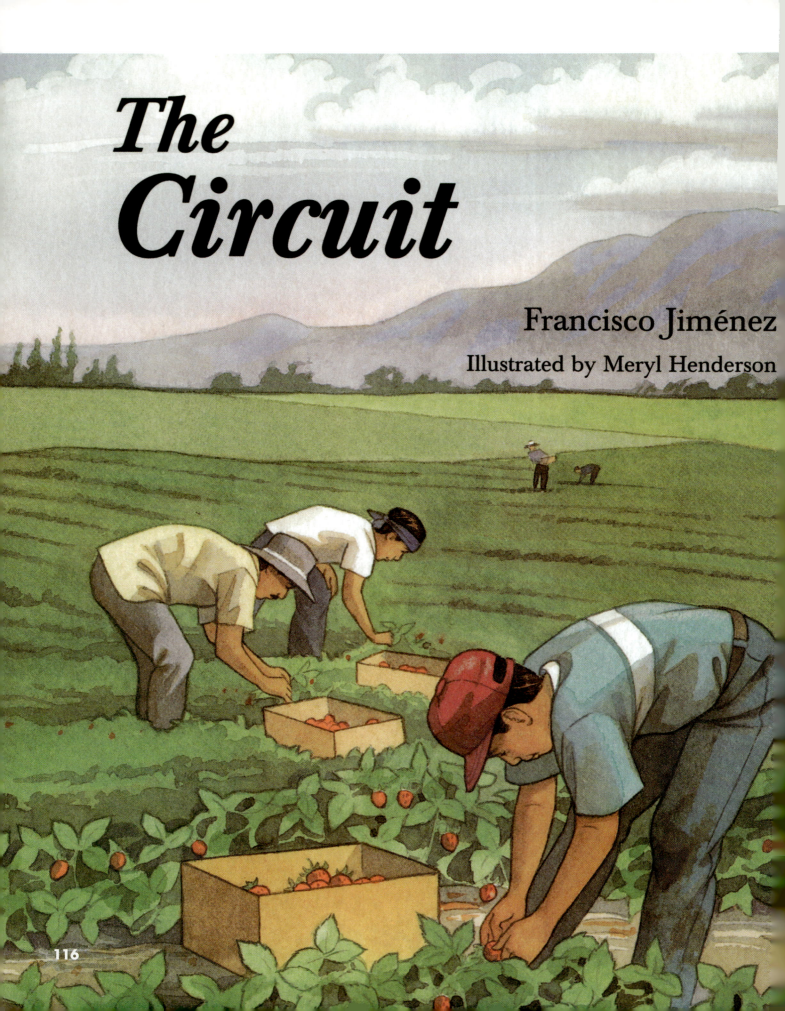

The Circuit

Francisco Jiménez

Illustrated by Meryl Henderson

It was that time of year again. Ito, the strawberry sharecropper, did not smile. It was natural. The peak of strawberry season was over and the last few days the workers, most of them *braceros,* were not picking as many boxes as they had during the months of June and July.

As the last days of August disappeared, so did the number of braceros. Sunday, only one—the best picker came to work. I liked him. Sometimes we talked during our half-hour lunch break. That is how I found out he was from Jalisco, the same state in Mexico my family was from. That Sunday was the last time I saw him.

When the sun had tired and sunk behind the mountains, Ito signaled us that it was time to go home. *"Ya esora,"* he yelled in his broken Spanish. Those were the words I waited for twelve hours a day, everyday, seven days a week, week after week. And the thought of not hearing them again saddened me.

As we drove home Papa did not say a word. With both hands on the wheel, he stared at the dirt road. My older brother, Roberto, was also silent. He leaned his head back and closed his eyes. Once in a while he cleared from his throat the dust that blew in from outside.

Yes, it was that time of year. When I opened the front door to the shack, I stopped. Everything we owned was neatly packed in cardboard boxes. Suddenly I felt even more the weight of hours, days, weeks, and months of work. I sat down on a box. The thought of having to move to Fresno and knowing what was in store for me there brought tears to my eyes.

That night I could not sleep. I lay in bed thinking about how much I hated this move.

A little before five o'clock in the morning, Papa woke everyone up. A few minutes later, the yelling and screaming of my little brothers and sisters, for whom the move was a great adventure, broke the silence of dawn. Shortly, the barking of dogs accompanied them.

While we packed the breakfast dishes, Papa went outside to start the "Carcanchita." That was the name Papa gave his old '38 black Plymouth. He bought it in a used-car lot in Santa Rosa in the winter of 1949. Papa was very proud of his little car. *"Mi Carcanchita,"* my little jalopy, he called it. He had a right to be proud of it. He spent a lot of time looking at other cars before buying this one. When he finally chose the "Carcanchita," he checked it thoroughly before driving it out of the car lot. He examined every inch of the car. He listened to the motor, tilting his head from side to side like a parrot, trying to detect any noises that spelled car trouble. After being satisfied with the looks and sounds of the car, Papa then insisted on knowing who the original owner was. He never did find out from the car salesman. But he bought the car anyway. Papa figured the original owner must have been an important man because behind the rear seat of the car he found a blue necktie.

Papa parked the car out in front and left the motor running. *"Listo"* (ready), he yelled. Without saying a word, Roberto and I began to carry the boxes out to the car. Roberto carried the two big boxes and I carried the two smaller ones. Papa then threw the mattress on top of the car and tied it with ropes to the front and rear bumpers.

Everything was packed except Mama's pot. It was an old large galvanized pot she had picked up at an army surplus store in Santa Maria the year I was born. The pot was full of dents and nicks, and the more dents and nicks it had, the more Mama liked it. *"Mi olla"* (my pot), she used to say proudly.

I held the front door open as Mama carefully carried out her pot by both handles, making sure not to spill the cooked beans. When she got to the car, Papa reached out to help her with it. Roberto opened the rear car door and Papa gently placed it on the floor behind the front seat. Papa sighed, wiped the sweat off his forehead with his sleeve, and said wearily, *"Es todo"* (that's it).

As we drove away, I felt a lump in my throat. I turned around and looked at our little shack for the last time.

At sunset we drove into a labor camp near Fresno. Since Papa did not speak English, Mama asked the camp foreman if he needed any more workers. "We don't need no more," said the foreman, scratching his head. "Check with Sullivan down the road. Can't miss him. He lives in a big white house with a fence around it."

When we got there, Mama walked up to the house. She went through a white gate, past a row of rose bushes, up the stairs to the front door. She rang the doorbell. The porch light came on and a tall husky man came out. They exchanged a few words. After the man went in, Mama clasped her hands and hurried back to the car. "We have work! Mr. Sullivan said we can stay there the whole season," she said gasping and pointing to an old garage near the stables.

The garage was worn out by the years. It had no windows. The walls, eaten by termites, strained to support the roof full of holes. The loose dirt floor, populated by earthworms, looked like a gray road map.

That night, by the light of a kerosene lamp, we unpacked and cleaned our new home. Roberto swept away the loose dirt, leaving the hard ground. Papa plugged the holes in the walls with old newspapers and tin cap tops. Mama fed my little brothers and sisters. Papa and Roberto then brought in the mattress and placed it on the far corner of the garage. "Mama, you and the little ones sleep on the mattress. Roberto, Panchito, and I will sleep outside under the trees," Papa said.

Early next morning Mr. Sullivan showed us where his crop was, and after breakfast, Papa, Roberto, and I headed for the vineyard to pick.

Around nine o'clock the temperature had risen to almost one hundred degrees. I was completely soaked in sweat and my mouth felt as if I had been chewing on a handkerchief. I walked over to the end of the row, picked up the jug of water we had brought, and began drinking. "Don't drink too much; you'll get sick," Roberto shouted. No sooner had he said that than I felt sick to my stomach. I dropped to my knees and let the jug roll off my hands. I remained motionless with my eyes glued on the hot sandy ground. All I could hear was the drone of insects. Slowly I began to recover. I poured water over my face and neck and watched the black mud run down my arms and hit the ground.

I still felt a little dizzy when we took a break to eat lunch. It was past two o'clock and we sat underneath a large walnut tree that was on the side of the road. While we ate, Papa jotted down the number of boxes we had picked. Roberto drew designs on the ground with a stick. Suddenly I noticed Papa's face turn pale as he looked down the road. "Here comes the school bus," he whispered loudly in alarm. Instinctively, Roberto and I ran and hid in the vineyards. We did not want to get in trouble for not going to school. The yellow bus stopped in front of Mr. Sullivan's house. Two neatly dressed boys about my age got off. They carried books under their arms. After they crossed the street, the bus drove away. Roberto and I came out from hiding and joined Papa. *"Tienen que tener cuidado"* (you have to be careful), he warned us.

After lunch we went back to work. The sun kept beating down. The buzzing insects, the wet sweat, and the hot dry dust made the afternoon seem to last forever. Finally the mountains around the valley reached out and swallowed the sun. Within an hour it was too dark to continue picking. The vines blanketed the grapes, making it difficult to see the bunches. *"Vámonos,"* said Papa, signaling to us that it was time to quit work. Papa then took out a pencil and began to figure out how much we had earned our first day. He wrote down numbers, crossed some out, wrote down some more. *"Quince"* (fifteen dollars), he murmured.

When we arrived home, we took a cold shower underneath a waterhose. We then sat down to eat dinner around some wooden crates that served as a table. Mama had cooked a special meal for us. We had rice and tortillas with *carne con chile*, my favorite dish.

The next morning I could hardly move. My body ached all over. I felt little control over my arms and legs. This feeling went on every morning for days until my muscles finally got used to the work.

It was Monday, the first week of November. The grape season was over and I could now go to school. I woke up early that morning and lay in bed, looking at the stars and savoring the thought of not going to work and of starting sixth grade for the first time that year. Since I could not sleep, I decided to get up and join Papa and Roberto at breakfast. I sat down at the table across from Roberto, but I kept my head down. I did not want to look up and face him. I knew he was sad. He was not going to school today. He was not going tomorrow, or next week, or next month. He would not go until the cotton season was over, and that was sometime in February. I rubbed my hands together and watched the dry, acid-stained skin fall to the floor in little rolls.

When Papa and Roberto left for work, I felt relief. I walked to the top of a small grade next to the shack and watched the "Carcanchita" disappear in the distance in a cloud of dust.

Two hours later, around eight o' clock, I stood by the side of the road waiting for school bus number twenty. When it arrived I climbed in. No one noticed me. Everyone was busy either talking or yelling. I sat in an empty seat in the back.

When the bus stopped in front of the school, I felt very nervous. I looked out the bus window and saw boys and girls carrying books under their arms. I felt empty. I put my hands in my pants pockets and walked to the principal's office. When I entered I heard a woman's voice say: "May I help you?" I was startled. I had not heard English for months. For a few seconds I remained speechless. I looked at the lady who waited for an answer. My first instinct was to answer in Spanish, but I held back. Finally, after struggling for English words I managed to tell her that I wanted to enroll in the sixth grade. After answering many questions, I was led to the classroom.

Mr. Lema, the sixth-grade teacher, greeted me and assigned me a desk. He then introduced me to the class. I was so nervous and scared at that moment when everyone's eyes were on me that I wished I were with Papa and Roberto picking cotton. After taking roll, Mr. Lema gave the class the assignment for the first hour.

"The first thing we have to do this morning is finish reading the story we began yesterday," he said enthusiastically. He walked up to me, handed me an English book, and asked me to read. "We are on page 125," he said politely. When I heard this, I felt blood rush to my head; I felt dizzy. "Would you like to read?" he asked hesitantly. I opened the book to page 125. My mouth was dry. My eyes began to water. I could not begin. "You can read later," Mr. Lema said understandingly.

For the rest of the reading period I kept getting angrier and angrier with myself. I should have read, I thought to myself.

During recess I went into the restroom and opened my English book to page 125. I began to read in a low voice, pretending I was in class. There were many words I did not know. I closed the book and headed back to the classroom.

Mr. Lema was sitting at his desk correcting papers. When I entered he looked up at me and smiled. I felt better. I walked up to him and asked if he could help me with the new words. "Gladly," he said.

The rest of the month I spent my lunch hours working on English with Mr. Lema, my best friend at school.

One Friday during lunch hour Mr. Lema asked me to take a walk with him to the music room. "Do you like music?" he asked me as we entered the building.

"Yes, I like Mexican *corridos*," I answered. He then picked up a trumpet, blew on it and handed it to me. The sound gave me goose bumps. I knew that sound. I heard it in many Mexican corridos. "How would you like to learn how to play it?" he asked. He must have read my face because before I could answer, he added: "I'll teach you how to play it during our lunch hours."

That day I could hardly wait to get home to tell Papa and Mama the great news. As I got off the bus, my little brothers and sisters ran up to meet me. They were yelling and screaming. I thought they were happy to see me, but when I opened the door to our shack, I saw that everything we owned was neatly packed in cardboard boxes.

Extending Comprehension

Story Questions

1. What were some of the difficulties the narrator's father and his sons faced when they went to work in the fields?
2. Name two places the family lived. Describe what the second place looked like when they moved in. Then describe how the family worked to improve that place.
3. Tell how the author lets us know that the narrator doesn't like to move.
4. Who made school a happy place for the narrator? Tell two things this person did that made the narrator feel good.
5. How do you think the narrator feels at the end of the story? Tell why he feels that way.
6. Explain why the title of the story is "The Circuit." Hint: a circuit is a circle.

Discussion Topics

1. The author uses interesting words and sentences to describe what the narrator sees and how he feels. Here are four sentences from the book. Discuss the meaning of each sentence. Tell which words make the sentences more interesting.
   - "When the sun had tired and sunk behind the mountains, Ito signaled us it was time to go."
   - "The mountains around the valley reached out and swallowed the sun."
   - "Suddenly, I felt even more the weight of hours, weeks, and months of work."
   - "I woke up early that morning and lay in bed, looking at the stars and savoring the thought of not going to work . . ."
2. Do you think the children who work in this story should be going to school? During your discussion, try to answer the following questions.
   - Why does the father make his boys hide when the school bus arrives?
   - Why doesn't the mother make the father let the boys go to school?
   - Why do you think the narrator finally got to go to school but his brother didn't?
   - Why do you think the narrator likes school so much?

Writing Ideas

1. Although we learn a lot about the family in the story, some important facts are missing:
   - The last name of the family
   - The first name of the narrator
   - The age of the narrator
   - Where the mother learned English
   - The number of little brothers and sisters in the family

   From what you have learned about the narrator and his family, write a paragraph about those missing facts. You can give him a new first name, but see if you can find it in the story.

2. The narrator wants to write a letter to Mr. Lema to explain why he did not come back to school, but the narrator is working and the family has no paper. Write this letter for him. Tell Mr. Lema how grateful you are for his help. Explain to him why you are not in his classroom. Tell him what you are doing and how you feel about your life outside of school.

SALMON COUNT

by Clifford E. Trafzer
Illustrated by Alex Bloch

New Vocabulary Words

1. subside
2. tipis
3. blot out
4. abruptly
5. welled up
6. elders
7. in accordance
8. course of action
9. absorbed in
10. arrogantly
11. grudgingly
12. strained
13. proposal
14. moral support
15. ritual
16. revolves around
17. retire to
18. agonizing
19. repress
20. abandon

Definitions

1. When something **subsides,** it becomes weaker.
2. **Tipis** are tents that some Native American tribes use.
3. **Blot out** is another way of saying *get rid of.*
4. **Abruptly** is another way of saying *suddenly.*
5. When a feeling is **welling** up in you, you are overcome with that feeling.
6. **Elders** are older people who are very important in their community.
7. **In accordance** is another way of saying *in agreement.*
8. A **course of action** is a way to do something.
9. When you are **absorbed in** something, all of your attention is focused on that thing.
10. When you act **arrogantly,** you act like you are more important than everyone else.
11. When you act **grudgingly,** you do something unwillingly.
12. **Strained** is another word for *tense.*
13. A **proposal** is a plan.
14. When you give someone **moral support,** you give that person encouragement.
15. A **ritual** is a customary way of doing something.
16. **Revolves around** is another way of saying *centers on.*
17. When you **retire to** a room, you go to that room to stay for a while.
18. Things that are **agonizing** cause agony and pain.
19. **Repress** is another way of saying *hold back.*
20. When you **abandon** something, you give up that thing.

Story Background

"Salmon Count" is another example of realistic fiction. The story is about the efforts of the Nez Perce (pronounced "nez purse") Native American tribe to get back their salmon fishing rights. These rights had been established in the Nez Perce Treaty of 1863. This treaty was an agreement between the Nez Perce, who live in Idaho, and the United States government. The treaty stated that the Nez Perce could fish for salmon wherever they had done so in the past. A treaty with the United States government has priority over state laws. This means that if a state's law says something different from what a treaty agreement says, you obey the treaty with the United States government instead of the state law.

Salmon play an important role in the Nez Perce culture. The tribe has a long tradition of catching salmon. The Nez Perce depend on salmon as a main source of food. Of course, people other than the Nez Perce also like to eat salmon. As a result, other people fish for salmon to sell or to eat. This creates problems because too many people are fishing for salmon. One problem is that the Nez Perce count on having salmon to eat to survive. Another problem is that if too many people fish for salmon, there won't be enough left in the rivers and salmon will eventually become extinct.

In the story, the state of Idaho has a law that says when people can go fishing. The state law, however, is in conflict with the treaty the Nez Perce have with the United States government. According to the treaty, the Nez Perce can fish wherever they want. On the other hand, the state law says that people living in Idaho can only fish for salmon at certain times of the year.

In the story, there is a preliminary trial in front of a judge because four of the Nez Perce have been arrested for breaking the state's fishing law. In a preliminary trial, a judge listens to both sides of a case and decides if there is enough evidence for a trial with a jury. In this story, the lawyer for the state, called the prosecutor, tries to prove that the four defendants are guilty because they broke the state law.

Many Native Americans have their own way of making important decisions. Members of the tribe gather together. These gatherings are called council meetings. In the story, the council holds a meeting to discuss what to do about the four tribal members who have been arrested and who must go to court. The council decides to hire a lawyer to prove that those who were arrested are innocent. The council wants the lawyer to prove that the four tribal members were following the treaty agreement. This lawyer is called the defense attorney because he defends those who have been arrested.

Focus Questions

- How did Matthew's mother set a good example when she found out her son had been arrested?
- What was Grandfather's role in the story—what was his purpose?
- What reasons did Matthew have to feel proud of himself, his mother, and his grandfather?
- What evidence did Mr. Cohen present to the judge?
- What important conversation occurred between Matthew and his grandfather at the end of the story?

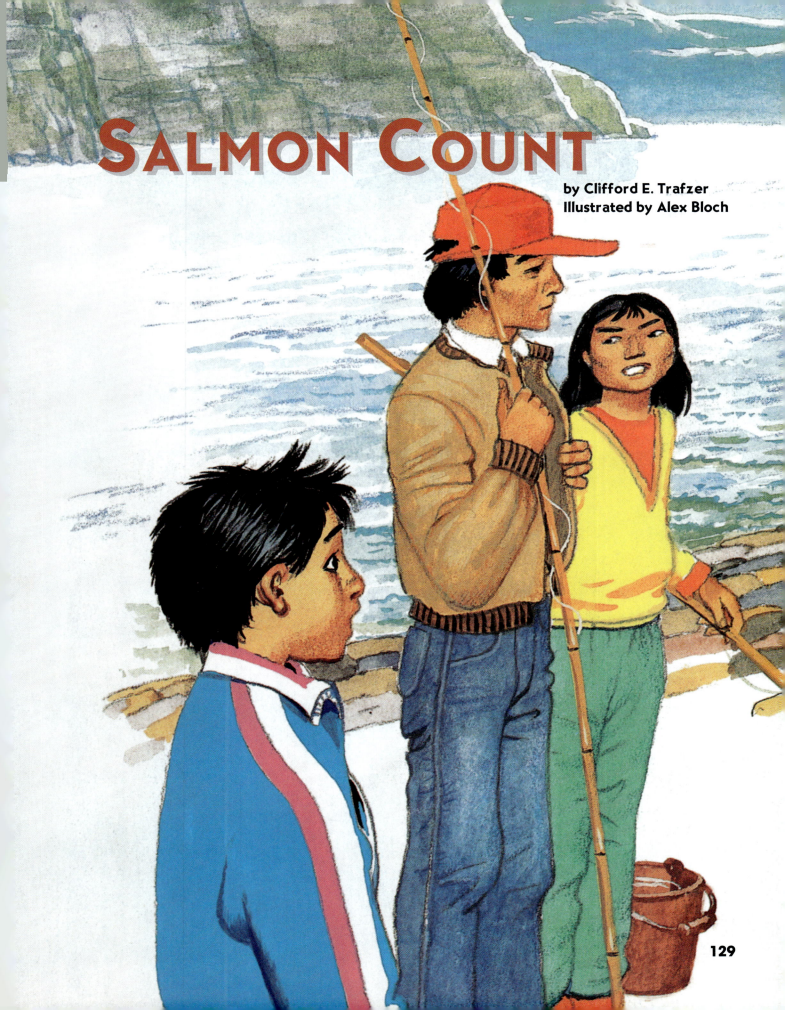

SALMON COUNT

by Clifford E. Trafzer
Illustrated by Alex Bloch

The sound of the handcuffs snapping shut around my brother's wrists echoed through the canyon. My stomach lurched and my throat closed into a dry lump. I was stunned by the sight of Matthew, wearing the red plaid shirt I had given him, being led away. That officer might as well have had no face. I remember only the brown uniform with bright brass buttons, the hat, and the silver-tinted sunglasses that hid the man's eyes. When Matthew tried to turn to say good-bye, he stumbled on the uneven ground. They passed out of view before I could move. Car doors slammed, the engine raced, and Matthew was gone.

The police also arrested Watie Jim, Wendell Scott, and Anna Hawk. They said our people were outlaws because they were fishing without a state fishing license. After that, our group stopped fishing. The camp was quiet for a time. Dazed, I walked along the Salmon River. I hiked a short distance to a rocky cliff overlooking the river. The pounding in my heart had subsided, but a dry lump still swelled in my throat. I sat down under a pine tree to collect my thoughts and wait for my mother's return. *She will be furious*, I thought.

Below me lay the six tipis we'd set up near the bank of the Salmon River. A group of small children played in the camp, shrieking and laughing as they chased each other. A few dogs added their sharp barks to the noise. Smoke drifted up from the smoldering campfires. I tried unsuccessfully to blot out the memory of police rushing toward us. The officers had yelled something, but we had not been able to make out their words over the roar of the river. Unsure of what to do, we had stood holding our fishing poles and watched them race forward.

"What happened, Andrew?" my mother asked when she returned, her arms filled with groceries. Her face wore that stern look that usually meant I had done something wrong. "What happened here?"

"The police came. They arrested Matt. They took Watie, Wendell, and Anna, too," I blurted out. My voice was shaking. I worried that my mother blamed me for allowing the police to take Matt. She reached out her small, sun-darkened hand, brushing my black hair away from my eyes.

"I'm glad they didn't take you," she said. "But we need to think of a way to get Matt back." She turned abruptly and walked swiftly back to camp.

Everything was in a stir. A crowd had gathered in the center of camp, and people were voicing their opinions about the arrests.

"We don't have to put up with this," I heard one man say. "These people have been doing this to Native Americans for years. I say we've taken it too long." As the crowd murmured its agreement, I felt a cloud of angry power sweep over us. My mother broke the spell.

"No one wants to get them back any more than I do." Her calm voice silenced the crowd. "But we can't act in anger." To my surprise, the group turned toward my mother. A feeling of pride welled up in me as I noticed people quieting down to listen. She knew the power of words, and she used them well that day.

"What will we win by using violence? We must be as wise as the elders who have taught us. We are *Nee Me Poo,* Nez Perce people. We must act in accordance with our traditions. We should go home and eat our supper. Later, we can meet here in council to decide the best course of action."

People nodded and began walking back to their lodges. My mother placed her arm around my shoulder, and we joined my grandfather and little sister. Grandfather had already begun cooking our meal of salmon, corn, beans, and bread. My mother and grandfather poured cups of steaming coffee for themselves, while my sister and I sipped cans of cold juice. Of course we talked about the arrests, anger filling our hearts and our words.

My grandfather spoke in a voice of quiet strength. "There was a time," he said, gazing into his coffee, "when the Nez Perce people took too many salmon." I looked at him with surprise. For a moment, I thought he might be joking. The people had always fished for salmon. It was their life! But as I studied his thin frame, his long gray hair, and his stern, wrinkled face, I knew he was serious.

"The old people say that we got greedy and took more salmon than we needed. That's when the Salmon People got together to meet in council. The men and women, even the children, sat down to talk about the situation." Grandfather paused to eat a chunk of salmon.

"The Salmon People knew they needed strong power. What they decided to do," Grandfather continued, wiping his hands on a napkin, "was to send Salmon Chief to visit Rattlesnake." I must have looked puzzled, because Grandfather addressed me directly.

He motioned toward me with his hand. "The Salmon Chief went to Rattlesnake hoping to get some of his power—his poison. Native Americans didn't bother Rattlesnake People because the rattlesnake had poison that could kill them. The Salmon People believed they could use the poison power to defend themselves."

Grandfather stood up, absorbed in his own story. He was not a tall man, but he seemed to tower over us. "Salmon Chief found Rattlesnake stretched out along the banks of Salmon River, sunning himself. 'Hello, brother,' Salmon called out, 'we are having some trouble here with the *Nee Me Poo* taking too many of us. So I have come to you, brother, to ask for some of your power.'

"At first Rattlesnake ignored Salmon Chief. Finally, he raised his head and looked down at Salmon Chief. 'I have no power to share with the Salmon People,' he said arrogantly. Salmon Chief was stung by the snake's refusal. In a fit of anger and frustration, the great chief lifted his tail and began beating Rattlesnake over the head.

"'Now will you give me some of your power?'" Grandfather imitated the Salmon Chief. "'No!' said Rattlesnake. Again, Salmon Chief beat him hard on the head. 'Now can we have some of your power?' Salmon Chief asked Rattlesnake. Again he was denied the poisonous power.

"Four times Salmon Chief asked Rattlesnake for his help," Grandfather continued with his story. "Only after the great Chief beat Rattlesnake five times on the head did the snake grudgingly give the Salmon People some of his power. That's why we are careful when we handle salmon. If he bites us, we will get infected with the poison given to Salmon People by Rattlesnake."

Grandfather smiled. "Have you ever wondered why the head of Rattlesnake is all smashed down?" he asked. "It is because of the time Salmon Chief beat Rattlesnake's head down flat."

My mother had listened to Grandfather's story respectfully. But when he finished, she said quietly, "Our people have always fished this river, Dad. No one can take that away from us." My grandfather nodded silently, but he directed a thoughtful glance my way. The strained exchange between my mother and my grandfather made me feel uncomfortable.

At the meeting everyone was given a chance to talk, even the young people like me. The woman next to me reminded us that the white man had destroyed the fish and that they now wanted to "protect" them. She told us that at the dams, the white people count every salmon that swims upriver, and that they want to decide how many fish we can catch. When she finished, it was my turn to speak. I was ready.

"In my class at school we have been studying Native American treaty rights. Our people made two treaties with the federal government, the Nez Perce Treaty of 1855 and the Nez Perce Treaty of 1863. I have read these treaties. We have talked about them in my class."

I paused for a moment to study the crowd. Men and women twice my age were listening carefully to my words. Encouraged by their attentiveness, I quickly continued. "Our first treaty says that the government guarantees our right to fish at all usual and accustomed areas. The government meant for us to catch fish as we always have, wherever we used to fish. Louis Cohen, a lawyer from Spokane, came to my class and told us so. I think we should call Mr. Cohen and ask him to defend my brother and his friends, and our treaty rights."

My words took the people by surprise. Even my mother seemed stunned by my proposal. I was beginning to feel a little embarrassed when Clarence Paul, one of our tribal leaders, stood up.

"Andrew's words are good," he announced. "I think he is on the right track. There is more at stake here than freeing our friends." Clarence's voice became louder. "We must make a stand against the state. They have no right, under our treaty, to stop us from fishing. Our agreement is with the United States, and the state government can't interfere. I know this Louis Cohen. He is a man of honor who works well with Native American people. I say, we should ask him for his help."

People nodded their heads in agreement, and a murmur of approval spread through the group. We invited Louis Cohen to defend my brother and his friends.

All along I was confident we would win the case. But on the day we went to the district court in Camasville, I was not so certain. Outside the courthouse on the rolling green lawn, five drums beat. Many singers gathered around the drums, singing some of the old songs. My heart soared hearing those songs. I was proud of the support these people were showing for my brother and the others.

The drumming finally ended, and everyone filed into the crowded courtroom. I sat nervously with the families of the defendants, in a row of seats located behind my brother and the others. Several people offered moral support by handing feathers and bundles to those on trial.

We all stood up when the judge entered the courtroom. Television made the routine seem eerily familiar, but this was not a TV show. My brother's freedom was at stake. Our freedom to live as we once lived was at stake. I watched nervously as the judge and attorneys began acting out the courtroom ritual. I knew this was only a preliminary trial, where the prosecuting attorney and the defense attorney would present their cases. The judge would determine if there was a need for a trial. The prosecutor made her case against the defendants, arguing that they were fishing off the reservation without a state fishing license. She said they had broken several laws.

Then, Mr. Cohen stood up, pausing dramatically before making his opening statement. He turned thoughtfully, gazing at the Native Americans filling the seats of the small courtroom. Slowly, he faced the judge, a white woman about 50 years old. The judge sat quietly throughout the opening statements by the prosecutor, now and then taking notes. An uneasy look passed over the judge's face. She squirmed slightly, swiveling her large leather chair. Mr. Cohen's hesitation seemed to be making her impatient and irritable.

Mr. Cohen finally spoke. "Your Honor," he began, "please allow me to offer a little background information that might clarify this matter." The judge nodded slightly, encouraging Mr. Cohen to continue. "Matthew George, Watie Jim, Wendell Scott, and Anna Hawk are Nez Perce Native Americans. Their people lived here on this land long before the arrival of Lewis and Clark or any other white people. Their lives, even their religion, revolve around their ties to this place. For centuries, the Nez Perce fished for salmon. Whenever they took the first salmon of the season, they held a thanksgiving ceremony called the First Salmon Ceremony. A strong bond exists between the defendants and the salmon."

Mr. Cohen paused and reached for several pieces of paper, holding them up for all to see. "Your Honor, I have in my hand the Nez Perce Treaty of 1855, a treaty offered by the national government to the Nez Perce. At the treaty council, Governor Isaac I. Stevens, who represented the United States, told the Nez Perce that forevermore the government would recognize their right to take fish at any time of year, on or off the reservation.

"Your Honor, I have offered to you this treaty and many other cases to show that the four defendants had a legal right to fish on the Salmon River. If you carefully consider the evidence and my arguments, you will find that the state has no case against the defendants. I hope you will then order their immediate release."

When the court session ended and the judge retired to her chambers, everyone remained seated. But when Mr. Cohen rose to leave the court, my mother and I stood up with the other Native Americans to show our respect for our attorney.

The days passed with agonizing slowness while we awaited the judge's decision. My family went through the motions of normal life, but my brother's legal battle remained foremost in our thoughts. Several days after the court hearing, I returned home hot and sweaty from a basketball game with some friends. My mother tried to look casual, but she couldn't repress her smile. I knew immediately that we had won.

As we hurried to the car to pick up Matthew, my mother turned to me. "You should be proud of yourself, Andrew," she said. "You helped us that day at the river."

Her words astonished me. "It was you who suggested that we call Mr. Cohen," my mother continued, "and it was you who said that our treaty rights were at stake. You helped us to see what we needed to do."

The glow from my mother's praise warmed me throughout the afternoon and into the evening. The family celebrated Matthew's homecoming with a meal of broiled salmon, green beans, boiled potatoes, and huckleberry pie. We talked long into the night, but Grandfather left shortly after supper. He slipped out of the house quietly, crossing our backyard to his little house. Dawn was breaking when I finally retired to my room. Peering out my window, I noticed Grandfather's light was on.

As I walked toward the tattered screen of his front door, I saw him sitting in an ancient wooden rocker. His gray hair gleamed in the lamplight, and long strands of hair reached below his narrow shoulders. Grandfather's dark eyes stared out a cracked window into the fading night. He turned when I came into his house, and his old face wore a sadness I could not understand. After all, Matthew had come home.

"What's wrong, Grandfather?" I asked. He bowed his head, staring at the floor. I waited patiently for the old man to speak.

"Are you glad that Matthew has come home?" he finally asked. Of course I was. He nodded. "I am happy too, that all four have been released."

"Then why do you look so sad?" I asked. His attitude almost made me angry. "This was a night to celebrate. You hardly said a thing at supper." Leaning forward in his chair, Grandfather motioned for me to sit down across from him.

"Andrew, throughout all of this legal business, I have been very worried," he said. "I feel sad because I think our people have forgotten an important point. I am an old man. I believe strongly in our fishing rights. But these rights were not given to us by the white man. The law that gives us the right to fish comes from the Creator, not the government. The old stories tell us that Coyote led the salmon upstream to spawn and die. Coyote brought us this gift, so that we might live. When we catch the fish, we stop and give thanks. We sing and celebrate with prayers and feasting. You have done it yourself."

I nodded. I was listening very hard.

"Because we are tied to this earth," Grandfather continued, "we have a special responsibility to the plants and animals. We must take care of them, so that they will take care of us." My grandfather sighed. "This is our way, Andrew. Through all of our fights for fishing rights, now and in the future, we must not forget the fish. The Salmon People are like our brothers and sisters, and we are their caretakers."

I moved closer to Grandfather, placing my hand on his shoulder. I assured the old man that I would not abandon the ways of the Nez Perce.

"That is good," he said, placing his hand on mine. "Tell your children and their children." He paused. "As long as there are young people like you, Andrew, I think our traditions will live for a long time."

We went outside and sat close together, quietly sharing the beginning of the new day.

Extending Comprehension
Story Questions

1. Why were the four Nez Perce arrested?
2. How did Matthew's mother react when she found out her son had been arrested?
3. What were some of the messages in the story Grandfather told about the Salmon People and Rattlesnake?
4. What did Andrew speak about at the council meeting?
5. What course of action did the tribe decide to take?
6. What was the background information that Mr. Cohen, the defendants' attorney, presented to the judge?
7. Why was Grandfather sad near the end of the story?

Discussion Topics

1. Andrew's grandfather was a wise man. He felt deeply about Nez Perce traditions. What were some things Grandfather did to make sure his tribe's traditions weren't forgotten? During your discussion, try to answer the following questions:
   - What was the main message of the legend about the Salmon People and Rattlesnake?
   - What "special responsibility" did Grandfather want Andrew to understand and carry on?

2. Pretend you are not a Nez Perce and you have to follow the state's laws about when you can fish. Do you agree with the judge's decision? During your discussion, try to answer the following questions:
   - Why should treaties that are over 100 years old still be legal?
   - Why should treaties that are over 100 years old not be legal?

Writing Ideas

1. One theme in this story is the importance of protecting the environment. Write a legend that sends this message.
2. Even though Andrew is a child, the adults in the tribe listened to his ideas. Why do you think it is important for adults to listen to children?
3. Pretend you are the lawyer for the state, the prosecuting attorney. Write a plan for what you will say to the judge in court.
4. Pretend you are the defense attorney for the four Nez Perce Native Americans who were arrested. Write a plan for what you will say to the judge in court.

The No-Guitar Blues

by Gary Soto
Illustrated by Anni Matsick

New Vocabulary Words

1. warehouseman
2. muscular
3. perpetual
4. stash
5. deceitful
6. zombie
7. confess
8. wicker
9. wrongdoing
10. freeway

Mexican foods:
- tortillas
- papas
- chorizo con huevos
- empanadas

Definitions

1. A **warehouseman** lifts and moves things in a warehouse.
2. Someone who is **muscular** has well developed muscles.
3. If something is **perpetual,** it never stops.
4. To **stash** something away is to put it in a secret place.
5. A **deceitful** person misleads other people by telling lies.
6. Someone who looks like a **zombie** looks like someone who is almost dead.
7. When you **confess** something, you admit you did that thing.
8. In some churches, a basket made of **wicker** is passed around for people to put money in.
9. A **wrongdoing** is an action that is against the rules.
10. A **freeway** is a highway with many lanes of traffic.
11. **Mexican foods: Tortillas** are like flat pancakes; **papas** are potatoes; **chorizo con huevos** is fried sausage with eggs; **empanadas** are little pies filled with meat.

Story Background

"The No-Guitar Blues" is a story about a young Mexican American boy who wants a guitar. He and his family live in California. "The Circuit," another story about a Mexican American boy who lives in California, appears earlier in this book. The two boys in these stories and their families are similar in some ways but very different in other ways. One way they are similar is the city in which they live or live near. The family in "The No-Guitar Blues" lives in the city of Fresno. The family in "The Circuit" lives for a while in a garage on a farm near Fresno.

Another way these families are similar is that they keep the culture of Mexico alive in their daily lives. Both boys enjoy eating the Mexican food their mothers prepare. Both boys are interested in learning to play musical instruments so they can play the kind of music that comes from Mexico.

When you read these stories you will find more similarities between the two boys and their two families. You will find many differences as well. One difference is how the story is told. The story in "The Circuit" is told *by* a young boy, but the story in "The No-Guitar Blues" is told *about* a young boy.

Music is important to people from all over the world. Many people from Mexico bring musical instruments with them when they come to the United States. They play the music of Mexico in their new homes. Fausto, the young boy in "The No-Guitar Blues," wants to learn to play the guitar so he can play in a rock band. But he wants to play in a Mexican-style rock band. Still, he talks about the Mexican music his parents like. They like *conjunto* (con HOON toe) music, which often includes *corridos* (core REE dos), or sad songs that tell stories.

The narrator in "The Circuit" wants to learn to play the trumpet. He loves the sound of a trumpet and has heard it in many Mexican *corridos*.

Focus Questions

- Why did Fausto want to learn to play the guitar?
- Why did Fausto want to earn money?
- Why did Fausto always have doubts about his plans?
- How did Fausto resolve his doubts?

The No-Guitar Blues
by Gary Soto
Illustrated by Anni Matsick

The moment Fausto saw the group Los Lobos on "American Bandstand," he knew exactly what he wanted to do with his life—play guitar. His eyes grew large with excitement as Los Lobos ground out a song while teenagers bounced off each other on the crowded dance floor.

He had watched "American Bandstand" for years and had heard Ray Camacho and the Teardrops at Romain Playground, but it had never occurred to him that he too might become a musician. That afternoon Fausto knew his mission in life: to play guitar in his own band; to sweat out his songs and prance around the stage; to make money and dress weird.

Fausto turned off the television set and walked outside, wondering how he could get enough money to buy a guitar. He couldn't ask his parents because they would just say, "Money doesn't grow on trees" or "What do you think we are, bankers?" And besides, they hated rock music. They were into the *conjunto* music of Lydia Mendoza, Flaco Jimenez, and Little Joe and La Familia. And, as Fausto recalled, the last album they bought was *The Chipmunks Sing Christmas Favorites.*

But what the heck, he'd give it a try. He returned inside and watched his mother make tortillas. He leaned against the kitchen counter, trying to work up the nerve to ask her for a guitar. Finally, he couldn't hold back any longer.

"Mom," he said, "I want a guitar for Christmas."

She looked up from rolling tortillas. "Honey, a guitar costs a lot of money."

147

"How 'bout for my birthday next year," he tried again.

"I can't promise," she said, turning back to her tortillas, "but we'll see."

Fausto walked back outside with a buttered tortilla. He knew his mother was right. His father was a warehouseman at Berven Rugs, where he made good money but not enough to buy everything his children wanted. Fausto decided to mow lawns to earn money, and was pushing the mower down the street before he realized it was winter and no one would hire him. He returned the mower and picked up a rake. He hopped onto his sister's bike (his had two flat tires) and rode north to the nicer section of Fresno in search of work. He went door-to-door, but after three hours he managed to get only one job, and not to rake leaves. He was asked to hurry down to the store to buy a loaf of bread, for which he received a grimy, dirt-caked quarter.

He also got an orange, which he ate sitting at the curb. While he was eating, a dog walked up and sniffed his leg. Fausto pushed him away and threw an orange peel skyward. The dog caught it and ate it in one gulp. The dog looked at Fausto and wagged his tail for more. Fausto tossed him a slice of orange, and the dog snapped it up and licked his lips.

"How come you like oranges, dog?"

The dog blinked a pair of sad eyes and whined.

"What's the matter? Cat got your tongue?" Fausto laughed at his joke and offered the dog another slice.

At that moment a dim light came on inside Fausto's head. He saw that it was sort of a fancy dog, a terrier or something, with dog tags and a shiny collar. And it looked well fed and healthy. In his neighborhood, the dogs were never licensed, and if they got sick they were placed near the water heater until they got well.

This dog looked like he belonged to rich people. Fausto cleaned his juice-sticky hands on his pants and got to his feet. The light in his head grew brighter. It just might work. He called the dog, patted its muscular back, and bent down to check the license.

"Great," he said. "There's an address."

The dog's name was Roger, which struck Fausto as weird because he'd never heard of a dog with a human name. Dogs should have names like Bomber, Freckles, Queenie, Killer, and Zero.

Fausto planned to take the dog home and collect a reward. He would say he had found Roger near the freeway. That would scare the daylights out of the owners, who would be so happy that they would probably give him a reward. He felt bad about lying, but the dog *was* loose. And it might even really be lost, because the address was six blocks away.

Fausto stashed the rake and his sister's bike behind a bush, and, tossing an orange peel every time Roger became distracted, walked the dog to his house. He hesitated on the porch until Roger began to scratch the door with a muddy paw. Fausto had come this far, so he figured he might as well go through with it. He knocked softly. When no one answered, he rang the doorbell. A man in a silky bathrobe and slippers opened the door and seemed confused by the sight of his dog and the boy.

"Sir," Fausto said, gripping Roger by the collar. "I found your dog by the freeway. His dog license says he lives here." Fausto looked down at the dog, then up to the man. "He does, doesn't he?"

The man stared at Fausto a long time before saying in a pleasant voice, "That's right." He pulled his robe tighter around him because of the cold and asked Fausto to come in. "So he was by the freeway?"

"Uh-huh."

"You bad, snoopy dog," said the man, wagging his finger. "You probably knocked over some trash cans, too, didn't you?"

Fausto didn't say anything. He looked around, amazed by this house with its shiny furniture and a television as large as the front window at home. Warm bread smells filled the air and music full of soft tinkling floated in from another room.

"Helen," the man called to the kitchen. "We have a visitor." His wife came into the living room wiping her hands on a dishtowel and smiling. "And who have we here?" she asked in one of the softest voices Fausto had ever heard.

"This young man said he found Roger near the freeway."

Fausto repeated his story to her while staring at a perpetual clock with a bell-shaped glass, the kind his aunt got when she celebrated her twenty-fifth anniversary. The lady frowned and said, wagging a finger at Roger, "Oh, you're a bad boy."

"It was very nice of you to bring Roger home," the man said. "Where do you live?"

"By that vacant lot on Olive," he said. "You know, by Brownie's Flower Place."

The wife looked at her husband, then Fausto. Her eyes twinkled triangles of light as she said, "Well, young man, you're probably hungry. How about a turnover?"

"What do I have to turn over?" Fausto asked, thinking she was talking about yard work or something like turning trays of dried raisins.

"No, no, dear, it's a pastry." She took him by the elbow and guided him to a kitchen that sparkled with copper pans and bright yellow wallpaper. She guided him to the kitchen table and gave him a tall glass of milk and something that looked like an *empanada*. Steamy waves of heat escaped when he tore it in two. He ate with both eyes on the man and woman who stood arm-in-arm smiling at him. They were strange, he thought. But nice.

"That was good," he said after he finished the turnover. "Did you make it, ma'am?"

"Yes, I did. Would you like another?"

"No, thank you. I have to go home now."

As Fausto walked to the door, the man opened his wallet and took out a bill. "This is for you," he said. "Roger is special to us, almost like a son."

Fausto looked at the bill and knew he was in trouble. Not with these nice folks or with his parents but with himself. How could he have been so deceitful? The dog wasn't lost. It was just having a fun Saturday walking around.

"I can't take that."

"You have to. You deserve it, believe me," the man said.

"No, I don't."

"Now don't be silly," said the lady. She took the bill from her husband and stuffed it into Fausto's shirt pocket. "You're a lovely child. Your parents are lucky to have you. Be good. And come to see us again, please."

Fausto went out, and the lady closed the door. Fausto clutched the bill through his shirt pocket. He felt like ringing the doorbell and begging them to please take the money back, but he knew they would refuse. He hurried away, and at the end of the block, pulled the bill from his shirt pocket: it was a crisp twenty-dollar bill.

"Oh, man, I shouldn't have lied," he said under his breath as he started up the street like a zombie. He wanted to run to church for Saturday confession, but it was past four-thirty, when confession stopped.

He returned to the bush where he had hidden the rake and his sister's bike and rode home slowly, not daring to touch the money in his pocket. At home, in the privacy of his room, he examined the twenty-dollar bill. He had never had so much money. It was probably enough to buy a secondhand guitar. But he felt bad, like the time he stole a dollar from the secret fold inside his older brother's wallet.

Fausto went outside and sat on the fence. "Yeah," he said. "I can probably get a guitar for twenty. Maybe at a yard sale—things are cheaper."

His mother called him to dinner.

The next day he dressed for church without anyone telling him. He was going to go to eight o'clock mass.

"I'm going to church, Mom," he said. His mother was in the kitchen cooking *papas* and *chorizo con huevos.* A pile of tortillas lay warm under a dishtowel.

"Oh, I'm so proud of you, Son." She beamed, turning over the crackling *papas.*

His older brother, Lawrence, who was at the table reading the funnies, mimicked, "Oh, I'm so proud of you, my son," under his breath.

At Saint Theresa's he sat near the front. When Father Jerry began by saying we are all sinners, Fausto thought he looked right at him. Could he know? Fausto fidgeted with guilt. No, he thought. I only did it yesterday.

Fausto knelt, prayed, and sang. But he couldn't forget the man and the lady, whose names he didn't even know, and the *empanada* they had given him. It had a strange name but tasted really good. He wondered how they got rich. And how that dome clock worked. He had asked his mother once how his aunt's clock worked. She said it just worked, the way the refrigerator works. It just did.

Fausto caught his mind wandering and tried to concentrate on his sins. He said a Hail Mary and sang, and when the wicker basket came his way, he stuck a hand reluctantly in his pocket and pulled out the twenty-dollar bill. He ironed it between his palms, and dropped it into the basket. The grown-ups stared. Here was a kid dropping twenty dollars in the basket, while they gave just three or four dollars.

There would be a second collection for Saint Vincent de Paul, the lector announced. The wicker baskets again floated in the pews, and this time the adults around him, given a second chance to show their charity, dug deep into their wallets and purses and dropped in fives and tens. This time Fausto tossed in the grimy quarter.

Fausto felt better after church. He went home and played football in the front yard with his brother and some neighbor kids. He felt cleared of wrongdoing and was so happy that he played one of his best games of football ever. On one play, he tore his good pants, which he knew he shouldn't have been wearing. For a second, while he examined the hole, he wished he hadn't given the twenty dollars away.

Man, I coulda bought me some Levi's, he thought. He pictured his twenty dollars being spent to buy church candles. He pictured a priest buying an armful of flowers with *his* money.

Fausto had to forget about getting a guitar. He spent the next day playing soccer in his good pants, which were now his old pants. But that night during dinner, his mother said she remembered seeing an old bass guitarron the last time she cleaned out her father's garage.

"It's a little dusty," his mom said, serving his favorite enchiladas, "But I think it works. Grandpa says it works."

Fausto's ears perked up. That was the same kind the guy in Los Lobos played. Instead of asking for the guitar, he waited for his mother to offer it to him. And she did, while gathering the dishes from the table.

"No, Mom, I'll do it," he said, hugging her. "I'll do the dishes forever if you want."

It was the happiest day of his life. No, it was the second-happiest day of his life. The happiest was when his grandfather Lupe placed the guitarron, which was nearly as huge as a washtub, in his arms. Fausto ran a thumb down the strings, which vibrated in his throat and chest. It sounded beautiful, deep and eerie. A pumpkin smile widened on his face.

"OK, *hijo*, now you put your fingers like this," said his grandfather, smelling of tobacco and aftershave. He took Fausto's fingers and placed them on the strings. Fausto strummed a chord on the guitarron, and the bass resounded in their chests.

The guitarron was more complicated than Fausto imagined. But he was confident that after a few more lessons he could start a band that would someday play on "American Bandstand" for the dancing crowds.

Extending Comprehension

Story Questions

1. Why did Fausto want to learn to play the guitar?
2. What are the first two ideas that Fausto had for earning money?
3. What made Fausto think Roger belonged to rich people?
4. Why did Fausto feel bad after the man gave him the money?
5. Why did Fausto decide to go to confession?
6. Tell why many of the people in the church put more money in the wicker basket the second time it went around.
7. Give at least two reasons why Fausto was happy at the end of the story.

Discussion Topics

1. "The No-Guitar Blues" begins and ends with descriptions of music and of playing musical instruments. Fausto wants to become a musician. Do you think he will succeed? Talk about what he would have to do to become a musician good enough to play in a group. During your discussion, try to answer the following questions:
   - What must people do to learn to play an instrument?
   - How do you think young people can learn to play in a group?
   - Would you like to be a musician? What kind?
   - Would you like to play in a group? In a band? In an orchestra?

2. After he took the $20 from the man, Fausto knew he had committed a wrongdoing. Before the story ends, Fausto finds a way to forgive himself. Discuss what he did and some other things he could have done. During your discussion, try to answer the following questions:
   - What does Fausto do to forgive himself?
   - What are some other things he could have done?
   - What would you have done?
   - Did Fausto learn something about himself by the end of the story?

Writing Ideas

1. Pretend a friend of Fausto's mother tells her that Fausto put $20 in the wicker basket at church. Fausto's mother asks him for an explanation. She wants to know where he got the $20 and why he gave it away. Pretend you are Fausto writing a letter of explanation to his mother. Tell why you needed money and the ideas you had for earning money. Then tell about Roger and what you decided to do with him. Describe the man and the woman and how the man gave you the $20. Then tell what made you decide that you shouldn't keep the $20 and what you decided to do so you would feel better.
2. Compare the families in "The Circuit" and "The No-Guitar Blues." Tell three ways the families are similar to each other, then tell three ways they are different from each other.
3. Write about a time you felt bad because you knew you had done something wrong. Then tell what you did to feel better.
4. The author says that the day that Fausto's grandfather placed the guitarron in his arms was the happiest day of Fausto's life. Write about one of the happiest days of your life. Tell what happened and why it made you feel happy.

Raymond's Run

by Toni Cade Bambara
Illustrated by Doris Ettlinger

New Vocabulary Words

1. playing the dozens
2. Mercury
3. island
4. prodigy
5. sidekicks
6. May Pole
7. corsages
8. bongos
9. periscope
10. gesture
11. psyching up
12. jutting out

Definitions

1. When kids are **playing the dozens,** they are trying to outwit each other.
2. **Mercury** is the name of a Roman god who travels swiftly. He is sometimes called Quicksilver.
3. In a city, an **island** is a safety zone in the middle of a busy street.
4. A young person with exceptional talent is a **prodigy.**
5. A **sidekick** is a very close friend.
6. A **May Pole** is a tall pole decorated with streamers. Children hold the streamers and dance around the pole.
7. A **corsage** is a small bouquet of flowers worn by a woman.
8. **Bongos** are a pair of connected drums that are beaten with the hands.
9. A **periscope** is an instrument that contains lenses and mirrors. These are arranged so people can get a view of something that is not in their direct line of vision.
10. When people use hand or body movements to express an idea or a feeling, they are making **gestures.**
11. When a runner is **psyching up** for a race, she gets herself mentally ready for the race.
12. Something that **juts out,** sticks out.

Story Background

The setting for "Raymond's Run" is New York City. Toni Cade Bambara, the author of this story, has spent most of her life in New York City. She writes stories and novels about the people who live there. Her characters do things that people do every day in New York City, and they talk like many of the people who live there.

New York City has the most people of any city in the United States. Over seven million people live in this city. If you look at a picture book of New York, you will see pictures of tall skyscrapers, big hotels, and beautiful parks. When you watch television shows that take place in New York, you sometimes see the beautiful offices of important people who are wearing expensive-looking clothes and the fancy apartments in which they live.

When Toni Cade Bambara writes about New York, she doesn't write about tall buildings and people who wear expensive clothes. Rather, she writes about lesser known parts of the city and about the lives of the everyday people who live, work, and play in these places. Like Mavis Jukes, who wrote "Like Jake and Me," Toni Cade Bambara writes realistic fiction for young people. In their stories, these authors create characters who may remind us of people we know. They write about events that may be similar to our own experiences.

If you live in a big city, you may feel right at home as you read "Raymond's Run." If you don't live in a big city, you may learn about the lives of young people who live in a big city. As you read the story, pay attention to the narrator and what she says about her family and her teachers and how she deals with the kids in her neighborhood.

The title, "Raymond's Run," contains the name of the narrator's brother. Although Raymond is older than his sister, their family puts her in charge of him. She is in charge of him because, as she says, "He's not quite right." We don't learn much more about how or why Raymond is not quite right, except that his head is big. We do learn that he walks down the street in an odd way but that his sister doesn't put up with anyone making fun of him. We also learn that he has a hidden talent, but we have to wait to the end of the story to find out what it is.

Focus Questions

- What is the narrator's nickname? Why does she have that name? What is her real name?
- What does the narrator say and do to let you know she is serious about running?
- Why is the narrator critical of Cynthia Proctor and the girls she meets on the sidewalk?
- What is the narrator's attitude toward dressing up for the May Pole dance and wearing a strawberry costume?
- What different things do you learn about Raymond as you read the story?
- How does what the narrator says about smiles at the end of the story change from what she said in the middle of the story?
- What happens at the end of the May Day race to make the narrator laugh out loud?

Raymond's Run

by Toni Cade Bambara
Illustrated by Doris Ettlinger

I don't have much work to do around the house like some girls. My mother does that. And I don't have to earn my pocket money by hustling; George runs errands for the big boys and sells Christmas cards. And anything else that's got to get done, my father does. All I have to do in life is mind my brother Raymond, which is enough.

Sometimes I slip and say my little brother Raymond. But as any fool can see he's much bigger and he's older too. But a lot of people call him my little brother cause he needs looking after cause he's not quite right. And a lot of smart mouths got lots to say about that too, especially when George was minding him. But now, if anybody has anything to say to Raymond, anything to say about his big head, they have to come by me. And I don't play the dozens or believe in standing around with somebody in my face doing a lot of talking. I much rather just knock you down and take my chances even if I am a little girl with skinny arms and a squeaky voice, which is how I got the name Squeaky. And if things get too rough, I run. And as anybody can tell you, I'm the fastest thing on two feet.

There is no track meet that I don't win the first place medal. I used to win the twenty-yard dash when I was a little kid in kindergarten. Nowadays, it's the fifty-yard dash. And tomorrow I'm subject to run the quarter-meter relay all by myself and come in first, second, and third. The big kids call me Mercury cause I'm the swiftest thing in the neighborhood. Everybody knows that—except two people who know better, my father and me. He can beat me to Amsterdam Avenue with me having a two fire-hydrant headstart and him running with his hands in his pockets and whistling. But that's private information. Cause you can imagine some thirty-five-year-old man stuffing himself into PAL shorts to race little kids? So as far as everyone's concerned, I'm the fastest and that goes for Gretchen, too, who has put out the tale that she is going to win the first-place medal this year. Ridiculous. In the second place, she's got short legs. In the third place, she's got freckles. In the first place, no one can beat me and that's all there is to it.

I'm standing on the corner admiring the weather and about to take a stroll down Broadway so I can practice my breathing exercises, and I've got Raymond walking on the inside close to the buildings, cause he's subject to fits of fantasy and starts thinking he's a circus performer and that the curb is a tightrope strung high in the air. And sometimes after a rain he likes to step down off his tightrope right into the gutter and slosh around getting his shoes and cuffs wet. Then I get hit when I get home. Or sometimes if you don't watch him he'll dash across traffic to the island in the middle of Broadway and give the pigeons a fit. Then I have to go behind him apologizing to all the old people sitting around trying to get some sun and getting all upset with the pigeons fluttering around them, scattering their newspapers and upsetting the waxpaper lunches in their laps. So I keep Raymond on the inside of me, and he plays like he's driving a stage coach which is O.K. by me so long as he doesn't run me over or interrupt my breathing exercises, which I have to do on account of I'm serious about my running, and I don't care who knows it.

Now some people like to act like things come easy to them, won't let on that they practice. Not me. I'll high-prance down 34th Street like a rodeo pony to keep my knees strong even if it does get my mother uptight so that she walks ahead like she's not with me, don't know me, is all by herself on a shopping trip, and I am somebody else's crazy child. Now you take Cynthia Procter for instance. She's just the opposite. If there's a test tomorrow, she'll say something like, "Oh, I guess I'll play handball this afternoon and watch television tonight," just to let you know she ain't thinking about the test. Or like last week when she won the spelling bee for the millionth time, "A good thing you got 'receive,' Squeaky, cause I would have got it wrong. I completely forgot about the spelling bee." And she'll clutch the lace on her blouse like it was a narrow escape. Oh, brother. But of course when I pass her house on my early morning trots around the block, she is practicing the scales on the piano over and over and over and over. Then in music class she always lets herself get bumped around so she falls accidentally on purpose onto the piano stool and is so surprised to find herself sitting there that she decides just for fun to try out the ole keys. And what do you know—Chopin's waltzes just spring out of her fingertips and she's the most surprised thing in the world. A regular prodigy. I could kill people like that. I stay up all night studying the words for the spelling bee. And you can see me any time of day practicing running. I never walk if I can trot, and shame on Raymond if he can't keep up. But of course he does, cause if he hangs back someone's liable to walk up to him and get smart, or take his allowance from him, or ask him where he got that great big pumpkin head. People are so stupid sometimes.

So I'm strolling down Broadway breathing out and breathing in on counts of seven, which is my lucky number, and here comes Gretchen and her sidekicks: Mary Louise, who used to be a friend of mine when she first moved to Harlem from Baltimore and got beat up by everybody till I took up for her on account of her mother and my mother used to sing in the same choir when they were young girls, but people ain't grateful, so now she hangs out with the new girl Gretchen and talks about me like a dog; and Rosie, who is as fat as I am skinny and has a big mouth where Raymond is concerned and is too stupid to know that there is not a big deal of difference between herself and Raymond and that she can't afford to throw stones. So they are steady coming up Broadway and I see right away that it's going to be one of those Dodge City scenes cause the street ain't that big and they're close to the buildings just as we are. First I think I'll step into the candy store and look over the new comics and let them pass. But that's chicken and I've got a reputation to consider. So then I think I'll just walk straight on through them or even over them if necessary. But as they get to me, they slow down. I'm ready to fight, cause like I said I don't feature a whole lot of chit-chat, I much prefer to just knock you down right from the jump and save everybody a lotta precious time.

"You signing up for the May Day races?" smiles Mary Louise, only it's not a smile at all. A dumb question like that doesn't deserve an answer. Besides, there's just me and Gretchen standing there really, so no use wasting my breath talking to shadows.

"I don't think you're going to win this time," says Rosie, trying to signify with her hands on her hips all salty, completely forgetting that I have whupped her behind many times for less salt than that.

"I always win cause I'm the best," I say straight at Gretchen who is, as far as I'm concerned, the only one talking in this ventriloquist-dummy routine. Gretchen smiles, but it's not a smile, and I'm thinking that girls never really smile at each other because they don't know how and don't want to know how and there's probably no one to teach us how, cause grown-up girls don't know either. Then they all look at Raymond who has just brought his mule team to a standstill. And they're about to see what trouble they can get into through him.

"What grade you in now, Raymond?"

"You got anything to say to my brother, you say it to me, Mary Louise Williams of Raggedy Town, Baltimore."

"What are you, his mother?" sasses Rosie.

"That's right, Fatso. And the next word out of anybody and I'll be *their* mother too." So they just stand there and Gretchen shifts from one leg to the other and so do they. Then Gretchen puts her hands on her hips and is about to say something with her freckle-face self but doesn't. Then she walks around me looking me up and down but keeps walking up Broadway, and her sidekicks follow her. So me and Raymond smile at each other and he says, "Gidyap" to his team and I continue with my breathing exercises, strolling down Broadway toward the ice man on 145th with not a care in the world cause I am Miss Quicksilver herself.

I take my time getting to the park on May Day because the track meet is the last thing on the program. The biggest thing on the program is the May Pole dancing, which I can do without, thank you, even if my mother thinks it's a shame I don't take part and act like a girl for a change. You'd think my mother'd be grateful not to have to make me a white organdy dress with a big satin sash and buy me new white baby-doll shoes that can't be taken out of the box till the big day. You'd think she'd be glad her daughter ain't out there prancing around a May Pole getting the new clothes all dirty and sweaty and trying to act like a fairy or a flower or whatever you're supposed to be when you should be trying to be yourself, whatever that is, which is, as far as I am concerned, a poor Black girl who really can't afford to buy shoes and a new dress you only wear once a lifetime cause it won't fit next year.

I was once a strawberry in a Hansel and Gretel pageant when I was in nursery school and didn't have no better sense than to dance on tiptoe with my arms in a circle over my head doing umbrella steps and being a perfect fool just so my mother and father could come dressed up and clap. You'd think they'd know better than to encourage that kind of nonsense. I am not a strawberry. I do not dance on my toes. I run. That is what I am all about. So I always come late to the May Day program, just in time to get my number pinned on and lay in the grass till they announce the fifty-yard dash.

I put Raymond in the little swings, which is a tight squeeze this year and will be impossible next year. Then I look around for Mr. Pearson, who pins the number on. I'm really looking for Gretchen if you want to know the truth, but she's not around. The park is jam-packed. Parents in hats and corsages and breast-pocket handkerchiefs peeking up. Kids in white dresses and light-blue suits. The parkees unfolding chairs and chasing the rowdy kids from Lenox as if they had no right to be there. The big guys with their caps on backwards, leaning against the fence swirling the basketballs on the tips of their fingers, waiting for all these crazy people to clear out the park so they can play. Most of the kids in my class are carrying bass drums and glockenspiels and flutes. You'd think they'd put a few bongos or something for real like that.

Then here comes Mr. Pearson with his clipboard and his cards and pencils and whistles and safety pins and fifty million other things he's always dropping all over the place with his clumsy self. He sticks out in a crowd because he's on stilts. We used to call him Jack and the Beanstalk to get him mad. But I'm the only one that can out run him and get away, and I'm too grown for that silliness now.

"Well, Squeaky," he says, checking my name off the list and handing me number seven and two pins. And I'm thinking he's got no right to call me Squeaky, if I can't call him Beanstalk.

"Hazel Elizabeth Deborah Parker," I correct him and tell him to write it down on his board.

"Well, Hazel Elizabeth Deborah Parker, going to give someone else a break this year?" I squint at him real hard to see if he is seriously thinking I should lose the race on purpose just to give someone else a break. "Only six girls running this time," he continues, shaking his head sadly like it's my fault all of New York didn't turn out in sneakers. "That new girl should give you a run for your money." He looks around the park for Gretchen like a periscope in a submarine movie. "Wouldn't it be a nice gesture if you were . . . ahhh . . ."

I give him such a look he couldn't finish putting that idea into words. Grownups got a lot of nerve sometimes. I pin number seven to myself and stomp away, I'm so burnt. And I go straight for the track and stretch out on the grass while the band winds up with "Oh, the Monkey Wrapped his Tail Around the Flag Pole," which my teacher calls by some other name. The man on the loudspeaker is calling everyone to the track and I'm on my back looking at the sky, trying to pretend I'm in the country, but I can't, because even grass in the city feels hard as sidewalk, and there's just no pretending you are anywhere but in a "concrete jungle" as my grandfather says.

The twenty-yard dash takes all of two minutes cause most of the little kids don't know no better than to run off the track or run the wrong way or run smack into the fence and fall down and cry. One little kid, though, has got the good sense to run straight for the white ribbon up ahead so he wins. Then the second-graders line up for the thirty-yard dash and I don't even bother to turn my head to watch cause Raphael Perez always wins. He wins before he even begins by psyching the runners, telling them they're going to trip on their shoelaces and fall on their faces or lose their shorts or something, which he doesn't really have to do since he is very fast, almost as fast as I am. After that is the forty-yard dash which I use to run when I was in first grade. Raymond is hollering from the swings cause he knows I'm about to do my thing cause the man on the loudspeaker announced the fifty-yard dash, although he might just as well be giving a recipe for angel food cake cause you can hardly make out what he's sayin for the static. I get up and slip off my sweat pants and then I see Gretchen standing at the starting line, kicking her legs out like a pro. Then as I get into place I see that ole Raymond is on line on the other side of the fence, bending down with his fingers on the ground just like he knew what he was doing. I was going to yell at him but then I didn't. It burns up your energy to holler.

Every time, just before I take off in a race, I always feel like I'm in a dream, the kind of dream you have when you're sick with fever and feel all hot and weightless. I dream I'm flying over a sandy beach in the early morning sun, kissing the leaves of the trees as I fly by. And there's always the smell of apples, just like in the country when I was little and used to think I was a choo-choo train, running through the fields of corn and chugging up the hill to the orchard. And all the time I'm dreaming this, I get lighter and lighter until I'm flying over the beach again, getting blown through the sky like a feather that weighs nothing at all. But once I spread my fingers in the dirt and crouch over the Get on Your Mark, the dream goes and I am solid again and am telling myself, Squeaky you must win, you must win, you are the fastest thing in the world, you can even beat your father up Amsterdam if you really try. And then I feel my weight coming back just behind my knees then down to my feet then into the earth and the pistol shot explodes in my blood and I am off and weightless again, flying past the other runners, my arms pumping up and down and the whole world is quiet except for the crunch as I zoom over the gravel in the track. I glance to my left and there is no one. To the right, a blurred Gretchen, who's got her chin jutting out as if it would win the race all by itself. And on the other side of the fence is Raymond with his arms down to his side and the palms tucked up behind him, running in his very own style, and it's the first time I ever saw that and I almost stop to watch my brother Raymond on his first run. But the white ribbon is bouncing toward me and I tear past it, racing into the distance till my feet with a mind of their own start digging up footfuls of dirt and brake me short. Then all the kids standing on the side pile on me, banging me on the back and slapping my head with their May Day programs, for I have won again and everybody on 151st Street can walk tall for another year.

"In first place . . ." the man on the loudspeaker is clear as a bell now. But then he pauses and the loudspeaker starts to whine. Then static. And I lean down to catch my breath and here comes Gretchen walking back, for she's overshot the finish line too, huffing and puffing with her hands on her hips taking it slow, breathing in steady time like a real pro and I sort of like her a little for the first time. "In first place . . . " and then three or four voices get all mixed up on the loudspeaker and I dig my sneaker into the grass and stare at Gretchen who's staring back, we both wondering just who did win. I can hear old Beanstalk arguing with the man on the loudspeaker and then a few others running their mouths about what the stopwatches say. Then I hear Raymond yanking at the fence to call me and I wave to shush him, but he keeps rattling the fence like a gorilla in a cage like in them gorilla movies, but then like a dancer or something he starts climbing up nice and easy but very fast. And it occurs to me, watching how smoothly he climbs hand over hand and remembering how he looked running with his arms down to his side and with the wind pulling his mouth back and his teeth showing and all, it occurred to me that Raymond would make a very fine runner. Doesn't he always keep up with me on my trots? And he surely knows how to breathe in counts of seven cause he's always doing it at the dinner table, which drives my brother George up the wall. And I'm smiling to beat the band cause if I've lost this race, or if me and Gretchen tied, or even if I've won, I can always retire as a runner and begin a whole new career as a coach with Raymond as my champion. After all, with a little more study I can beat Cynthia and her phony self at the spelling bee. And if I bugged my mother, I could get piano lessons and become a star. And I have a big rep as the baddest thing around. And I've got a roomful of ribbons and medals and awards. But what has Raymond got to call his own?

So I stand there with my new plans, laughing out loud by this time as Raymond jumps down from the fence and runs over with his teeth showing and his arms down to the side, which no one before him has quite mastered as a running style. And by the time he comes over I'm jumping up and down so glad to see him—my brother Raymond, a great runner in the family tradition. But of course everyone thinks I'm jumping up and down because the men on the loudspeaker have finally gotten themselves together and compared notes and are announcing, "In first place—Miss Hazel Elizabeth Deborah Parker." (Dig that.) "In second place—Miss Gretchen P. Lewis." And I look over at Gretchen wondering what the "P" stands for. And I smile. Cause she's good, no doubt about it. Maybe she'd like to help me coach Raymond; she obviously is serious about running, as any fool can see. And she nods to congratulate me and then she smiles. And I smile. We stand there with this big smile of respect between us. It's about as real a smile as girls can do for each other, considering we don't practice real smiling every day, you know, cause maybe we too busy being flowers or fairies or strawberries instead of something honest and worthy of respect . . . you know . . . like being people.

Extending Comprehension

Story Questions

1. In what ways does Squeaky watch out for Raymond? Describe three events from the story that show how she takes care of him.
2. How does Squeaky let you know she is serious about running? Give two examples from the story.
3. Why is Squeaky critical of Cynthia Proctor and the girls she meets on the sidewalk?
4. How does Squeaky feel about dressing up for the May Pole dance and wearing a strawberry costume? Tell how she feels and why she feels that way.
5. Describe one thing Raymond is doing at the beginning of the story and one thing he is doing at the end of the story.
6. In the middle of the story, what does Squeaky say about the smiles of girls she knows? What does she say about smiles at the end of the story?
7. What happens at the May Day race to make Squeaky think about changing her plans?

Discussion Topics

1. Squeaky uses lots of **colorful language** to describe the people she knows and the neighborhood in which she lives. Some quotations from the story appear below. Break up into groups. Take turns reading what Squeaky says. Then discuss what she is talking about.

   - "The big kids call me Mercury cause I'm the swiftest thing in the neighborhood."

   - "He can beat me to Amsterdam Avenue with a two fire-hydrant headstart."

   - "I've got Raymond walking on the inside close to the building, cause he's subject to fits of fantasy and starts thinking he's a circus performer and that the curb is a tightrope strung high in the air.

   - "I'll high-prance down 34th Street like a rodeo pony to keep my knees strong."

   - "Sometimes, if you don't watch him, he'll dash across traffic to the island in the middle of Broadway and give the pigeons a fit."

   - "I'm on my back, looking at the sky, trying to pretend I'm in the country, but I can't because even grass in the city feels hard as sidewalk, and there's just no pretending you are anywhere but in a 'concrete jungle' as my grandfather says."

   After you discuss the meanings of these quotations, look in the story to find at least one more colorful quotation. Each person should read his or her quotation and then lead a discussion of that quotation.

2. When Gretchen and her sidekicks meet Squeaky and Raymond on the sidewalk, Squeaky says that Gretchen smiles but that girls never really smile. She also says girls don't know how to smile because grown-ups don't know how to smile either. Discuss these observations. During your discussion, try to answer the following questions:
   - Why does Squeaky claim girls never really smile?
   - Do you think she is right? Tell why.
   - Why does she believe girls aren't taught to smile?
   - Can you think of a time you had to smile but really didn't want to? Tell what happened.
   - What causes Squeaky to think she and Gretchen gave each other real smiles at the end of the race?

Writing Ideas

1. Toni Cade Bambara writes as if the narrator, Squeaky, is talking to someone she knows. Squeaky lets you know what she thinks of herself and what she thinks of other people. Pretend it is the day after the race. Squeaky meets Cynthia Proctor. Write about their conversation. Include what Squeaky tells about the race and what she learned about herself. Then write what you think Cynthia said to her. Write so it sounds like Squeaky and Cynthia are talking to each other.

2. You have been asked to write an article about the events of the May Day program for your school newspaper. Describe the park and the crowd of people who are there to watch the dancers and the racers. Tell about the May Pole dance, the little kids' run, the second-graders' run, and the 50-yard dash. Write about your interviews with Squeaky and Gretchen after the race.

3. Squeaky tells us what she thinks about just before she takes off in a race. Think about a time you were getting ready for something important. What did you think about just before you started? Write about what you did and how you got yourself ready to do it.

4. Write a story about next year's race. Raymond, Squeaky, and Gretchen are in the race, as well as other runners. You can decide who is in the race, what happens during the race, and who wins the race.

STORY 12
AFTER LESSON 120

Without a Shirt

by Paul Jennings
Illustrated by Kate Flanagan

New Vocabulary Words

1. smirk
2. rubbish
3. mussels
4. caretaker
5. pension
6. gale
7. spade

Definitions

1. A **smirk** is the kind of smile you give when you are making fun of someone or teasing someone in an unkind way.
2. **Rubbish** is another word for *garbage*.
3. **Mussels** are a type of seafood that are similar to clams.
4. A **caretaker** is someone who takes care of a place or another person.
5. A **pension** is money you get from an employer when you stop working or when the person you are married to dies.
6. A **gale** is a very strong wind.
7. A **spade** is a type of shovel.

Story Background

"Without a Shirt" is a ghost story that takes place in Australia. Even though people from Australia speak English, they sometimes use different words than people from the United States use to describe the same thing. Some of these words are similar, like Mum for Mom. But some of the words are not at all similar. See if you can figure out what the words from Australia mean by reading the sentences that follow.

- *When our guests arrived, we invited them to come in and sit on the sofa in the lounge.* What room do you think a lounge is?

- *George's mum is very rich. She wears very nice clothes and fancy jewelry and speaks in a posh voice.* What kind of voice is a posh voice?

- *After we finished shopping, we put the big bags in the boot of our car so there would be room in the back seat.* What part of a car do you think the boot is?

You will probably notice something else that is different in this story that lets you know the author is Australian. There are no periods after abbreviations like Mr. and Mrs., so they look like this: Mr Bush and Mrs Featherstone.

Focus Questions

- What extra words does Brian say before he stops talking?
- What does Shovel start to find after Brian and his mom move to the house at the cemetery?
- What happens the second time Brian tries to give his speech about his great-great-grandfather?
- What happens so that Brian stops saying extra words at the end of his sentences?

Without A Shirt

by Paul Jennings
Illustrated by Kate Flanagan

Mr Bush looked at the class. "Brian Bell, he said. "You can be the first one to give your History talk."

My heart sank. I felt sick inside. I didn't want to do it; I hated talking in front of the class. "Yes, Mr Bush without a shirt," I said. Sue Featherstone (daughter of the mayor) giggled. Slowly I walked out to the front of the class. I felt like death warmed up. My mouth was dry. "I am going to talk about my great great grandfather," I said. "He was a sailor. He brought supplies to Warrnambool in his boat without a shirt."

Thirty pairs of eyes were looking at me. Sue Featherstone was grinning. "Why didn't he wear a shirt?" she asked. She knew the answer. She knew all right. She just wanted to hear me say it.

"His name was Byron. People called him Old Ben Byron without a shirt."

"Why did they call him Old Ben Byron without a shirt?" Sue asked with a smirk. "That's a funny name."

"Don't tease him," said Mr Bush. "He is doing his best."

She was a mean girl, that Sue Featherstone. Real mean. She knew I couldn't help saying "without a shirt." After I had finished saying something I always said "without a shirt." All my life I had done it—I just couldn't help it. Don't ask me why. I don't know why; I just couldn't stop myself. I had been to dozens of doctors. None of them knew what caused it and none of them could cure me. I hated doing it. Everyone laughed. They thought I was a bit queer.

I looked at Sue Featherstone. "Don't be mean," I said. "Stop stirring. You know I can't stop saying 'without a shirt' without a shirt."

The whole grade cracked up. A lot of the kids tried not to laugh, but they just couldn't stop. They thought it was very funny. I went red in the face. I wished I was dead—and I wished that Sue Featherstone was dead too. She was the worst one in the form. She was always picking on me.

"Okay, Brian," said Mr Bush. "You can do your talk on Wednesday. You might be feeling a bit better by then." I went and sat down. Mr Bush felt sorry for me. They all felt sorry for me. Everyone except Sue Featherstone, that is. She never thought about anyone except herself.

PART 2

I walked home from school with Shovel. Shovel is my dog. He is called Shovel because he loves to dig holes. Nothing can stop him digging holes. He digs up old rubbish and brings it home and leaves it on the doorstep.

Once the man next door went fishing. He had a sack of mussels which he used for bait. When he got home he left them in the boot of his car and forgot about them. Two weeks later he found them—or I should say they found him. What a stink. Boy, were they on the nose! He had to bury them in his back yard. The next day Shovel dug them up and brought them home for me. He was always giving me presents like that. I didn't have the heart to punish him; he meant well. I just patted him on the head and said, "Good boy without a shirt."

Shovel was a great dog—terrific in fact. I am the first to admit that he didn't look much. He only had one eye, and half of one ear was gone. And he was always scratching. That wasn't his fault. It was the fleas. I just couldn't get rid of the fleas. I bought flea collars but they didn't work. I think that was because Shovel loved to roll in cow manure so much.

Apart from those few little things you wouldn't find a better dog than Shovel. He was always friendly and loved to jump up on you and give you a lick on the face. Mum and I would never give him up. He was all that we had left to remember Dad by. Shovel used to belong to Dad once. But Dad was killed in a car accident. So now there was just me, and Shovel and Mum.

When I reached home I locked Shovel in the back yard. It didn't look much like a back yard, more like a battle field with bomb holes all over it. Shovel had dug holes everywhere. It was no good filling them in; he would just dig them out again. I went into the kitchen to get a drink. I could hear Mum talking to someone in the lounge. It was Mrs Featherstone (wife of the mayor). She owned our house. We rented it from her. She was tall and skinny and had blue hair. She always wore a long string of pearls (real) and spoke in a posh voice.

"Mrs Bell," she was saying. "I'm afraid you will have to find another place to live. It just won't do. That dog has dug holes everywhere. The back yard looks like the surface of the moon. Either you get rid of the dog or you leave this house."

"We couldn't do that," said Mum. "Brian loves that dog. And it used to belong to his father. No, we couldn't give Shovel away."

Just then Shovel appeared at the window. He had something in his mouth. "There is the dreadful creature now," said Mrs Featherstone. "And what's that in its mouth?"

I rushed into the room. "Don't worry," I said. "It's only Tibbles without a shirt."

"Tibbles?" squeaked Mrs Featherstone. "What is Tibbles?"

"Our cat," I told her. "It died six months ago and I buried it at the bottom of the yard without a shirt."

Mrs Featherstone screamed and then she fainted. I don't know what all the fuss was about. It was only a dead cat. I know that Tibbles didn't look quite the same as when she was alive, but was that any reason to go and faint?

Anyhow, that is how we got kicked out of our house. And that is why we had to go and live in the cemetery.

PART 3

When I say that we had to live in a cemetery I don't mean that we lived in a grave or anything like that. No, we lived in a house in the middle of the cemetery. It was a big, dark old house. Once the caretaker lived there, but he was gone now and no one else wanted to live in it. That's why the rent was cheap. It was all that we could afford. Mum was on the pension and we didn't have much money.

"You'll be happy here," said the estate agent to Mum. "It's very quiet. And it's the cheapest house in town."

"I don't think that anyone can be happy in a graveyard," said Mum. "But it will have to do for now. It's all we can afford."

The agent walked off to his car. He was smiling about something. Then he looked at Shovel. "I hope your dog doesn't dig holes," he said. "It's not a good idea for dogs that live in cemeteries to dig holes." He thought that he had said something really funny. He was still laughing as he drove out of the gate.

"Big joke without a shirt," I called out after him.

The next day we moved in. I had a little room at the top of the house. I looked out over the graves. I could see the sea close by. The cemetery was next to the beach—we just had to walk over the sand dunes and there we were at Lady Bay Beach.

I went up to my room and started to work on my talk for school. I decided to write the whole thing out. That way I could make sure that I didn't have any "without a shirts" in it. I didn't want to give Sue Featherstone the chance to laugh at me again. The only trouble was that the last time I tried this it didn't work. I still said the "without a shirts" anyway. Still, it was worth a try—it might work this time. This is what I wrote.

OLD BEN BYRON

Old Ben Byron was my great great grandfather. He was the captain of a sailing ship. He sailed in with all sorts of goods for the town. He was one of the early settlers. This town is only here because of men like Ben Byron.

One day a man fell overboard. My great great grandfather jumped over to help him. The man was saved. But old Ben Byron was swept away. He drowned. His body was never found.

I know this might seem a bit short for a talk at school. It is. But something happened that stopped me writing any more.

Shovel had been gone for some time; I was starting to worry about him. I hoped he wasn't scratching around near any of the graves. I looked out the window and saw him coming. I ran downstairs and let him in. He ran straight up to my room and dropped something on the floor. It was a bone.

PART 4

I picked up the bone and looked at it. It was very small and pointed—just one little white bone. I could tell it was old. I knew I had seen a bone like that somewhere before, but I just couldn't think where. A funny feeling started to come over me. I felt lonely and lost, all alone. I felt as if I was dead and under the sea, rolling over and over.

My hand started to shake and I dropped the bone. I stared down at the bone on the floor. I was in bare feet and the bone had fallen right next to my little toe. Then I knew what sort of bone it was—it was a bone from someone's toe. It was a human toe bone.

"Oh no," I said to Shovel. "What have you done? Where have you been digging? You bad dog. You have dug up a grave. Now we are in trouble. Big trouble. If anyone finds out we will be thrown out of this house. We will have nowhere to live without a shirt."

I put on my shoes and ran outside. The strange feeling left me as soon as I closed the bedroom door. I only felt sad when I was near the bone. Outside it was cold and windy. I could hear the high seas crashing on the other side of the sand dunes. "Show me where you got it," I yelled at Shovel. "Show me which grave it was without a shirt." Shovel didn't seem to listen; he ran off over the sand dunes to the beach and left me on my own. I looked at all the graves. There were thousands and thousands of them. It was a very old cemetery and most of the graves were overgrown.

I started walking from one grave to the other trying to find signs of digging. I searched all afternoon. But I found nothing. I couldn't find the place where Shovel had dug up the bone.

In the end I walked sadly back to the house. I didn't know what to do with the bone. If anyone found it there would be a terrible fuss. We would be forced to leave the cemetery and would have nowhere to live.

When I reached the house Shovel was waiting for me. He was wagging his tail. He looked pleased with himself. He was covered in sand, and in his mouth he had another tiny bone. "The beach," I shouted. "You found it at the beach without a shirt." I snatched the bone from Shovel. As soon as I touched the bone the same sad feeling came over me. I felt lost and alone. I wanted something but I didn't know what it was.

It was another toe bone. I carried it up to my room and put it next to the other one. The feeling of sadness grew less. "That's strange without a shirt," I said to Shovel. I picked up the second bone and put it outside the door. The feeling came back. It was very strong. I opened the door and put the two bones together again. I didn't feel quite so sad. "These bones are not happy unless they are together," I said. "They want to be together without a shirt."

PART 5

I decided to have a serious talk to Shovel. I took his head between my hands. "Listen," I said. "You have to show me where you found these bones. I will have to fill in the hole. You can't go digging up dead bodies all over the place. You just can't without a shirt." Shovel looked at me with that big brown eye. I had the feeling that Shovel knew more about this than I did. He ran over to the door and started scratching at it. "Okay," I told him. "I'll come with you. But first I will hide these bones without a shirt." I put the two toe bones in a drawer with my socks. They still felt sad. So did I. As soon as I closed the drawer the feeling went.

We headed off to the beach. It was blowing a gale. The sand blew into my eyes and ears. I didn't know what to expect—maybe a big hole that Shovel had dug, with a skeleton in the bottom. Maybe a body washed up on the beach.

We climbed over the sand dunes and down to the shore. There was no one else on the beach. It was too cold. "Well," I said to Shovel, "show me where you got the bones without a shirt." He ran off into the sand dunes to a small hole. It was only as deep as my hand. There was no grave, just this small hole. I dug around with my hand but there were no other bones. "That's good," I told Shovel. "There is no grave, and there is no body. Just two toe bones. Tomorrow I will bury them and that will be the end of it without a shirt."

Shovel didn't listen. He ran off to the other end of the beach. It was a long way but I decided to follow him. When I reached him he was digging another hole. He found two more toe bones. I picked them up and straight away the sad, sad feeling came over me. "They want to be with the others," I said. "See if you can find any more without a shirt."

Shovel ran from one end of the beach to the other. He dug about thirty holes. In each hole he found one or two bones; some of them were quite big. I found an old plastic bag on the beach and put the bones in it. By the time it was dark the bag was full of unhappy bones. I felt like crying and I didn't know why. Even Shovel was sad. His tail was drooping. There wasn't one wag left in it.

I started to walk up the sand dunes towards home. Shovel didn't want to go; he started digging one more hole. It was a deep hole. He disappeared right inside it. At last he came out with something in his mouth, but it wasn't a bone. It was a shoe—a very old shoe. It wasn't anything like the shoes you buy in the shops. It had a gold buckle on the top. I couldn't see it properly in the dark. I wanted to take it home and have a good look at it.

"Come on, Shovel," I said. "Let's go home. Mum will be wondering where we are without a shirt." I picked up the bag and we walked slowly back to the house.

PART 6

I put the toe bones in the bag with the rest of them. Then I put the bag in my cupboard and shut the door. I felt much happier when the bones were locked away. They were unhappy and they made me unhappy. I knew what the trouble was; they wanted to be with all the other bones. I guessed that they were all buried in different places along the beach.

I looked at the shoe; it was all twisted and old. It had been buried in the sand dunes for a long time. I wondered whose it was. Then I noticed something—two initials were carved into the bottom. I could just read them. They were "B.B."

"Ben Byron," I shouted. "The bones belong to my great great grandfather without a shirt."

I suddenly thought of something—Ben Byron's shoe had reminded me. Tomorrow was Wednesday; I had to give my history talk at school. I groaned. I knew that I wouldn't be able to sleep worrying about it. And the more I worried the more nervous I would get. The more nervous I got the worse I would feel. The last time I gave a talk at school I got one out of ten. One out of ten. You couldn't get much lower than that.

Then I had an idea—I would take along the shoe. I would tell everyone I had found Ben Byron's shoe. That would make it interesting. I might even get three out of ten for my talk if I had the shoe. I put the shoe in my sock drawer and took the bag of bones out of the cupboard. I wanted to have a closer look at them.

I tipped the bones out into a pile on the floor. There were three long bones and a lot of small ones. The sad, lonely feeling came over me once more. I sat down on the bed and looked at the pile of sad bones. Then something happened that gave me a shock. The hair stood up on the back of my neck. I couldn't believe what I was seeing—the bones were moving. They were slowly moving around the floor. The bones were creeping around each other like a pile of snakes.

The bones sorted themselves out. They all fitted together. They formed themselves into a foot and a leg. All the bones were in the right order. I had the skeleton of Ben Byron's leg.

The leg didn't move. It just lay there on the floor. I sat on the bed looking at it for a long time. I can tell you I was scared—very scared. But I couldn't just leave the leg there; Mum might come in and see it. Anyway it was creepy having the skeleton of someone's leg lying on your bedroom floor. In the end I jumped up and swept all of the bones back into the bag and threw it into the corner of the room. Then I climbed into bed and put my head under the blanket. I tried to pretend that the bones weren't there.

PART 7

The next day I had to give my talk at school. It went worse than I thought. It was terrible. I stood in front of the class for ages without saying anything. I was so scared that my knees were knocking. The words just wouldn't come out. "What's up," said Sue Featherstone. "Haven't you got any shirts today?" A big laugh went up.

I managed to read the whole thing through to the end. I tried not to say anything else. I could feel it building up inside me—it was like a bomb waiting to go off. I kept my mouth closed tight but the words were trying to get out. My cheeks blew out and my face went red. "Look at him," laughed Sue Featherstone. "He's trying not to say it."

It was no good. The words exploded out. "Without a shirt."

I was embarrassed. I didn't know what to do. I grabbed the shoe. "This is Ben Byron's shoe," I said. "It was washed ashore without a shirt."

"It is not," said Sue Featherstone. "It's an old shoe that you found at the dump."

Everything was going wrong. I would probably get nought out of ten for this talk. Then something happened that changed everything. A feeling of sadness swept over me. Everyone in the room felt it—they all felt sad. Then someone screamed. It was the leg—it was standing there at the door. It hopped across the room. My hands were shaking so much that I dropped the shoe. The leg hopped across the platform and into the shoe. It wanted the shoe.

Sue Featherstone looked at the skeleton leg and started shouting out. "Get rid of it. Get rid of the horrible thing."

The leg started hopping towards her. It hopped right up onto her desk. She screamed and screamed. Then she ran for the door. Everyone else had the same idea—they all ran for the door at the same time. There was a lot of yelling and pushing. They were all trying to get out of the door at once. They were scared out of their wits.

The leg bones chased the whole class across the playground and down the street. I have never heard so much yelling and screaming in all my life.

I was left alone in the classroom with Mr Bush. He just sat there shaking his head. After a while he said, "I don't know how you did it, Brian. But it was a good trick. I give you ten out of ten for that talk. Ten out of ten."

"Thanks Mr Bush without a shirt," I said.

PART 8

When I got home from school the leg was waiting for me. It was just standing there in the corner of my room; it didn't move at all. But it was so sad and it made me sad. I felt as if I were a skeleton myself. I felt as if my bones were being washed away by the waves, as if they were being scattered along a long, sandy beach. I knew that this is what happened to Ben Byron. His bones had been washed up and scattered along Lady Bay Beach.

I looked at Shovel. "We have to find the rest of the bones," I said. "This leg will never have peace until all the bones are together again. We have to find the rest of the bones and we have to find them now without a shirt."

I took a spade and a sack and walked towards the beach. Shovel came with me and so did the leg. It hopped slowly behind us making a plopping sound as it came. It still had the shoe on. It was lucky that there was no one on the beach—they wouldn't have believed their eyes if they had seen a boy, a dog and a skeleton leg walking along the beach. I could hardly believe it myself.

I didn't know where to start looking. But the leg did. It hopped across the beach and stood still where it wanted us to dig. We spent all afternoon following the leg around and digging holes. In every hole we found some bones. I went as fast as I could; I wanted to get rid of the sad feeling. Tears were running down my face because I was so unhappy. Every time I found some more bones I put them in the sack. The bones were glad to be together; I could tell that. But they were still sad. They would not be happy until I found the last one.

After a long time I found the last bone. It was the skull. It was in a hole with an old shirt—a very old shirt. I had never seen one like it before. I put the skull and the shirt in the sack. Then I held open the top. The leg hopped into the sack with the other bones.

PART 9

The feeling of sadness went as soon as the leg joined the other bones. The bones were happy, I was happy and so was Shovel.

"Now," I said to Shovel. "We have a job to do. We have to bury all the bones in the same hole without a shirt."

I carried the bag of happy bones to a lonely place in the sand dunes, and Shovel and I started to dig a hole. We worked at it for hours and hours. At last it was deep enough. I took the bag of bones and tipped them into the grave. They fell into a pile out the bottom; then they started to move. They slithered around at the bottom of the hole. I should have felt scared but I didn't. I knew what was happening. The bones were joining up into a skeleton. After a while it was finished. The skeleton was whole. It lay still at the bottom of the grave looking up at me. It didn't look as if it was at peace. There was something else—it wanted something else. I looked in the sack. The shirt was still there.

I threw the shirt into the hole. "Don't worry," I said. "I won't bury you without a shirt."

The bones started to move for the last time. The skeleton moved onto its side with the shirt under its head. It was in a sleeping position. It was very happy. Music seemed to come up out of the grave—silent music. I could hear it inside my head.

We filled in the grave and smoothed down the sand. I decided to say a few words; after all, it was a sort of a funeral. I looked out to sea. I could feel tears in my eyes. This is what I said. "Here lie the bones of Ben Byron. At peace at last. Beside this beautiful bay."

Shovel looked up at me. He seemed to be smiling.

"Hey," I yelled. "I didn't mention a shirt. I didn't say it."

And I never did again.

Extending Comprehension

Story Questions

1. What problem did Brian Bell have when he spoke?
2. Brian felt sad each time Shovel dug up a bone and gave it to him. How else did he feel when this happened?
3. What shocked Brian when he poured all the bones out of the bag and onto the floor of his room?
4. What happened the second time Brian gave his speech at school about his great-great-grandfather?
5. What did Brian do to make the bones happy?

Discussion Topics

1. Discuss why you think this story is called "Without a Shirt." During your discussion, try to answer the following questions:
   - Why do you think the author has Brian say "without a shirt" before he stops talking?
   - When and why does Brian stop saying "without a shirt"?
2. "Without a Shirt" is a ghost story. Ghost stories are supposed to scare you.
   - Discuss the parts you thought were the scariest.
   - Discuss why you thought those parts were scary.

Writing Ideas

1. Pretend you are Old Ben Byron. Write a letter to your great-great-grandson Brian explaining what happened the day you died trying to save the man who fell overboard. Also, tell Brian how you feel now that he has found your bones and properly buried them with a shirt.
2. Throughout most of the story, it seems very strange for Brian to say extra words before he stops talking. These words never made any sense to anyone, including Brian. The last time Brian says "without a shirt" is near the end of the story. Here is what he says, "Don't worry, I won't bury you without a shirt." Why is this the last time Brian ends a sentence with these words?

Additional Reading

Ribsy
Section 1 (Chapter 1)
Word List

Beatrice
corduroy
galoshes
Henry Huggins
infuriate
intersection
Klickitat Street
menacing
persistent
Pomeranian
Ribsy
upholstery
color-blind
enthusiasm
half-hearted
imprisonment
initiative
jingle
lubricating oil
mutt
perspire
Ramona
sociable
whimper

Questions

1. Why was Ribsy always trying to scratch his neck?
2. Which paw did Ribsy use when he shook hands?
3. Why did Mrs. Huggins want Ribsy to stay out of the new car?
4. What did Ribsy do when the family drove off without him?
5. Why did Mrs. Huggins finally agree to let Ribsy come into the car?
6. What did Henry do to help Ribsy scratch his neck?
7. What kind of place did Mr. Huggins drive to?
8. Before Henry left Ribsy in the car, he opened the windows a little bit. Why did Henry do that?
9. Why did Ribsy try to get out of the car?
10. How was Ribsy able to open the window?
11. Which sense did Ribsy use when he tried to find Henry?
12. Why did Ribsy think that the blue station wagon might be Henry's car?
13. The book says that all dogs are color-blind. What does that mean?
14. Why was Ribsy so unhappy at the end of the chapter?

Section 2 (Chapter 2-3)
Word List

advertise
bewildered
crochet
doily
furnace
gunnysack
intention
master of ceremonies
Mrs. Frawley
pedigree
rhinestone
Subdivision
Tattletale
Valuable
under the circumstances
beseech
billow
Dingley
footsore
glum
Humane Society
investigate
mongrel
obedient
provoke
sill
sympathetic
thorough
violets

Questions

1. Why did the Dingley children decide to give Ribsy a bath?
2. George poured a bottle of something over Ribsy. What was it and what did it smell like?
3. Why did Ribsy keep dashing around and around the Dingley's house?
4. Why did Mr. Dingley stick Ribsy in the shower?
5. For a while, Ribsy could smell nothing but violets. Explain why that was dangerous for Ribsy.
6. After he ran away from the Dingleys, how did Ribsy try to get rid of the violet smell?

7. What did Henry do to let people know he had lost his dog?
8. What could Ribsy do that made him different from other dogs?
9. Which smell told Ribsy that Mrs. Frawley was cooking breakfast?
10. Why was Mrs. Frawley so happy to take care of Ribsy?
11. What important message was in the newspaper that the old gentleman carried?
12. What problems did Ribsy have at Mrs. Frawley's house?
13. Why did each lady bring something special to the club meeting?
14. What reasons did Ribsy have for wanting to escape from Mrs. Frawley?

Section 3 (Chapter 4-5)

Word List

adorable	allegiance
apologetic	appetizing
cafeteria	chicken pox
cloud of exhaust	corrugated
crepe paper	delirious
disappearance	discontinue
discouraged	elude
exception	grasp the situation
hair's breadth	Junior
mascot	obliging
pathetic	patriotic
pompons	S. P. C. A.
southpaw	stadium
stimulating	supplementary
surround	undamaged
uproar	vigil
warily	wistful

Questions

1. Who did Ribsy follow to the school?
2. When Ribsy first got to the school, why did all the students chase him?
3. Whose classroom did Ribsy end up in?
4. What did Ribsy do during the flag salute?
5. Why do you think the teacher let Ribsy become a member of the class?
6. What did Ribsy do as soon as the squirrel got out of the box?
7. How did the nurse finally catch the squirrel?
8. Why did Ribsy have to leave the school?
9. Ribsy came to a place that had gates and an enormous gray wall. What kind of place was that?
10. What wonderful smell came from that place?
11. How did Ribsy fool the man at the gate?
12. Why was Ribsy able to become choosy about what he ate?
13. Explain how Ribsy won the game for Taylor High.
14. Why did Joe Saylor claim that Ribsy was his dog?

Section 4 (Chapter 6-7)

Word List

absentminded	triumphant
barrette	apartment house
body-and-fender shop	bicker
	bologna
commotion	consist
dawdle	evict
exasperating	experimental
fire	gobble
escape	linger
interval	margarine
macaroni	receipt
mouth organ	saddlebag
retrieve	sensation
scornful	strenuous
snappish	

Questions

1. What was Darlene doing when Joe brought Ribsy home?
2. Do you think that the Saylors had a lot of extra money? Why or why not?
3. Explain why Ribsy began to feel that he belonged to Joe.
4. What did Darlene do to annoy Joe while he was watching TV?
5. How did Henry find out that Joe had Ribsy?
6. At first, why didn't Joe want to give Ribsy back to Henry?
7. What did Henry offer that made Joe change his mind?
8. Why did Ribsy become confused when Henry spoke to him on the phone?
9. Why did Ribsy run away from the Saylors?
10. What kind of building did Larry live in?
11. Larry was playing with something that interested Ribsy. What was that?
12. What was the "small square room without windows" that Larry took Ribsy into?
13. Where did Larry hide Ribsy?
14. Why was it so difficult for Ribsy to walk around his hiding place?
15. Describe how Henry's father finally rescued Ribsy.

Writing Assignment

Think about where you live. First write a paragraph that explains what it looks, sounds, and smells like to you. Then write another paragraph that explains what it might look, sound, and smell like to a dog.

Jennifer, Hecate, Macbeth ...
Section 1 (Chapters 1-3)
Word List

apartment house	apprentice
auditorium	avalanche
Cinerama	detention
estate	glamorous
greenhouse	hand-me-down
petticoat	Pilgrim
poetic license	postpone
Roman numeral	

Questions

1. At the beginning of the novel, why were Jennifer and Elizabeth wearing costumes?
2. How was Jennifer's costume different from Elizabeth's?
3. What kind of person did Jennifer claim to be?
4. Why did all the adults like Cynthia so much?
5. Why did Elizabeth dislike Cynthia?
6. What did Jennifer do to Cynthia's costume?
7. What was unusual about the way that Jennifer walked across the stage?
8. What was unusual about Jennifer's manners?
9. Why did Jennifer always bring an empty bag to people's doors when she went trick-or-treating?
10. Jennifer decided to make Elizabeth an ⬚ witch.
11. Why did Jennifer and Elizabeth hold a ceremony in the park?
12. What did Elizabeth have to eat every day for the next week?
13. Do you think that Jennifer is really a witch? Why or why not?

Section 2 (Chapters 4-5)

Word List

colonial
democratic
guillotine
janitor
Mrs. Stuyvestant
rehearsal
spontaneous
combustion
DDT
frolic
ingredient
Mona Lisa
ointment
renew a book

Questions

1. Why did the librarian like Jennifer?
2. Why did Elizabeth eat the special foods every week, even though she didn't like some of them?
3. Why did the girls decide against making an ointment that would change them into animals?
4. What kind of ointment did the girls decide to make instead?
5. How do you think Elizabeth felt about the story of the play? Why?
6. Why do you think Cynthia got to be the princess in the play?
7. Why did Elizabeth have to play the dog?
8. Why did Cynthia get sick when Elizabeth snuggled up to her?
9. How had Cynthia really brought the mixer to school?
10. What was Jennifer planning to do with the pot she brought to school?
11. Explain what Jennifer's "Ugh!!!" note meant.

Section 3 (Chapters 6-7)

Word List

accurate
cryptography
invitation
mastication
noticeable
parings
pronounce
taboo
boa constrictor
digestion
journeyman
mature
parakeet
precaution
sauerkraut
witch doctor

Questions

1. Why do you think Christmas might be a dangerous time of year for witches?
2. Why would it be easy to give up eating watermelon around Christmas?
3. When Elizabeth found the watermelon, what did that prove to her?
4. What kinds of foods did the Greats eat?
5. How did the Greats talk?
6. What happened when Elizabeth tried to put a spell on Cynthia?
7. Jennifer promoted Elizabeth from an apprentice to a _____ witch.
8. Describe some of the taboos that Elizabeth had to follow.
9. Why did Elizabeth refuse to cut her hair for the party?
10. Why did Elizabeth pretend she had a limp at the party?
11. When Cynthia was opening presents, why were the other girls so impressed with Elizabeth?
12. What was the secret behind Elizabeth's trick?
13. Why did Elizabeth step on Cynthia's foot?

Section 4 (Chapters 8-10)
Word List

cauldron
competent
sentimental
venom
commuter
Macbeth
tortoise

Questions

1. What was the name of the girls' toad?
2. How did the toad end up with such an unusual name?
3. How had the witches in *Macbeth* used a toad?
4. How did the girls plan to use the toad?
5. What was the first part of the warning that Jennifer gave Elizabeth?
6. Explain how the first part of the warning came true.
7. When the ointment was almost ready, why did Elizabeth make Jennifer stop?
8. Do you think that Jennifer wanted the toad to die? Why or why not?
9. How had Jennifer been able to get watermelon in January?
10. What happened to the girls after they stopped pretending to be witches?

Writing Assignment

Jennifer did some things that seemed magical.

Make a list of the magic-seeming things that Jennifer did. Then write a paragraph that explains how she really did them.

Island of the Blue Dolphins
Section 1 (Chapters 1-8)
Word List

abalone
Aleut
awl
bobbed about
canyon
carcass
Chowig
cormorant
custom
dune
fling
Ghalas-at
idle
Karana
lair
mesa
parley
ponder
ravine
school of fish
shirk
skim the water
sparingly
stride off
thrust
toyon bush
vow
yucca
abound
ample
bales
canoe
Captain Orlov
chieftain
clatter
council
decree
fateful
forlorn
gorge yourself
intruder
kelp
manhood
otter
pelts
perish
Ramo
scan
sea-elephant
shroud
slink
spit of land
switch of nettles
tide pool
two leagues long
webbed feet

Questions

1. What animal did the island look like?
2. Why did the Aleuts come to the island?
3. What was the bargain that Captain Orlov made with Chief Chowig?
4. Should Chowig have tried to make friends with the Aleuts? Why or why not?

5. Why did the Aleuts try to leave without telling Chowig?
6. What did Captain Orlov offer Chowig instead of the otter pelts?
7. What happened after Chowig refused Captain Orlov's offer?
8. The next year, some white men came to the island. How did the white men know about the people on the island?
9. What did the white men plan to do?
10. Why did Karana dive off the white men's ship?
11. What animals stole all the food from the village?
12. Early in the morning, Ramo left the hut to get something. What was that?
13. Why didn't Ramo get to where he was going?
14. What are some of the dangers that Karana will now have to face by herself?

Section 2 (Chapters 9-14)
Word List

ancestor	bellow
bowstring	brackish
chafe	cholla bush
clamor	crevice
ember	headland
legend	omen
pelican	pursue
quarrel	scarce
serpent	sinew
smother	stalking around
stunted	thrust
tusk	utensil

Questions

1. At first, why was Karana worried about making her own weapons?
2. What did Karana hope to find in the chest?
3. Why do you think she threw the bracelets into the ocean?
4. What reasons did Karana have for leaving the island?
5. When she left the island, what place did she hope to find?
6. What made her turn around and come back?
7. Which animals guided her back?
8. What objects did Karana use to build a fence?
9. What large object formed the back of Karana's house?
10. Why did Karana want to get the teeth of a sea elephant?
11. Describe how Karana was finally able to get the sea elephant's teeth.
12. When did Karana hurt her leg?
13. When she went to the spring, Karana found a new place to live. What kind of place was that?
14. Why do you think Karana wants to kill the wild dogs so much?

Section 3 (Chapters 15-20)
Word List

barbed
lupines
muzzle
scallop
ten paces
whine
haunch
matted fur
Rontu
sea urchin
warily

Questions

1. Why do you think Rontu was the leader of the wild dogs?
2. How did Karana wound Rontu?
3. Why do you think Rontu decided to stay with Karana?
4. Describe at least two ways in which Rontu and Karana helped each other.
5. What reasons did Karana have for repairing the canoe?
6. Where did Karana hide the canoe at night?
7. What did Karana plan to use the special spear for?
8. Why do you think Rontu went off to fight the two dogs?
9. How did Karana make sure that her pet birds would not fly away?
10. Karana called one animal a devilfish. What is the modern name for that animal?
11. Do you think it was smart of Karana to try to catch the devilfish? Why or why not?
12. Why did Karana move to the cave?
13. Why did she make her old house look so deserted?

Section 4 (Chapters 21-29)
Word List

circlet
olivella shell
snare
thong
fledgling
reproachfully
strewn

Questions

1. How did Karana feel when Tutok first discovered her?
2. Do you think that Rontu might really have been Tutok's dog? Why or why not?
3. Why did Karana leave the cave the night after Tutok discovered her?
4. What made Karana change her feelings about Tutok?
5. Karana had mixed feelings when the Aleuts left. Explain why.
6. Name some of the animals that Karana tamed or became friends with.
7. Why did Karana decide to stop killing certain animals?
8. During the summer, the otter would leave Coral Cove. Why?
9. Describe how Karana caught Rontu-Aru.
10. What kinds of things happened during the earthquake?
11. Why did Karana have to build a new canoe?
12. How did Karana communicate with the white men?
13. Why do you think Karana wanted to wear her cormorant skirt when she left the island?

Writing Assignment

Pretend that you are preparing to live by yourself on an island. Write a list of the things you will take with you. Then write a paragraph that explains all the things you plan to do on the island.

The Trumpet of the Swan

Section 1 (Chapters 1-6)

Word List

absence	ammunition
altitude	boggy
ascent	burble
bulrush	caboose
burrow	ceaselessly
caper	commotion
commonsense	compel
compass	endearment
diversion	exalted
escapade	existence
exhibition	intruder
idyllic	locate
irksome	majestic
locomotive	moose
masterpiece	offensive
odious	pangs of hunger
onerous	pellet
partridge	preen
peninsula	rasping
proportion	resonant
recreation	restful
responsibility	retreat
retract	revelation
riding the range	sensation
spellbound	stealthy
supreme	swamp
taken aback	taxi a plane
torture	unspoiled
utmost	victory
vigilant	vixen
adjacent	

Questions

1. In which country did this part of the novel take place?
2. Describe the area around the pond.
3. Why couldn't Sam and his father drive a car to their cabin?
4. In which season did the cob and his wife arrive at the pond?
5. The cob and his wife had different ways of speaking.
   a. What kinds of words did the cob use when he spoke?
   b. What were the cob's speeches like?
   c. What were his wife's speeches like?
6. How did Sam prove to the swans that he was their friend?
7. Why did the cob's wife build a nest?
8. What important defect did Louis have?
9. What was the cob thinking of getting for Louis?
10. What are the two meanings of the word *dumb*?
11. Why was it so funny when the cob said that there weren't many good listeners?
12. Why couldn't the swans stay at the pond all year long?
13. What kind of book did Sam write in every night?
14. Sam tried to answer a new question every day. What does that tell you about Sam?

Section 2 (Chapters 7-12)

Word List

ado	Serena
bale of hay	snicker
bugle	society
communicate	straggle
convertible	tarnish
countenance	valuable
desirous	waterfowl
disregard	antics
doleful	behavior
furthermore	captivity
hippie	consist
kingfisher	counselor
law-abiding	deplorable
Mrs. Hammerbotham	disinclined
	distinguished
noose	extraordinary
ovation	game warden
pursuit	impractical
rap for order	kooky
reveille	malodorous
sanctuary	nigh

outdistance
presentation
quest
reputation
sacrifice
sensibility
serenity
snippety
solitary
substitute
trustworthy
wallop

Questions

1. Why did Louis want to learn to read and write?
2. Where did Louis learn to read and write?
3. Explain how Louis communicated with people.
4. Why couldn't the other swans understand what Louis was trying to say?
5. How did Louis feel about Serena?
6. At first, why wasn't Serena interested in Louis?
7. Why did the cob decide to get a trumpet for Louis?
8. Explain how the cob got the trumpet.
9. Why did Louis need to earn money?
10. Why did Louis have a hard time flying?
11. How did Louis earn money?
12. What is taps?
13. Describe what Camp Kookooskoos looked like.
14. Why did Applegate become so upset?
15. So what did Applegate do?
16. Why did Louis get a medal?
17. Why was Louis a little unhappy when he got the medal?

Section 3 (Chapters 13-17)

Word List

acquaintance
armadillo
boarded up
canebrakes
composer
employment
favorable
gale
immaculate
irresistible
lighthearted
passionate
pinion
proposition
serene
surgery
throbbing
ungrateful
watercress
apathy
bide your time
bullfrog
celebrity
ecstasy
fashionable
felicity
hoist
independent
kidnap
paddle wheel
Philadelphia
popularity
revulsion
splashdown
symphony
orchestra
uncertainty
valve

Questions

1. What did Louis need to do before he could play the valves on his trumpet?
2. Describe Louis's job in Boston.
3. Why was the Boatman so happy to have Louis?
4. At first, why didn't the clerk want Louis to stay at the Ritz?
5. Why do you think Louis slept in a bathtub?
6. What did Louis order for dinner?
7. Why do you think the boatman decided to let Louis sleep on the lake?
8. Why did Louis lose his job in Boston?
9. To which city did Louis go next?
10. What was his job in that city?
11. How did the zoo keep the birds on the lagoon from flying away?

12. Why did Louis have to give a free concert each Sunday?
13. How did Serena end up in the lagoon?
14. What was the first song that Louis played for Serena?
15. How did Serena feel about Louis after she heard him play?
16. How is love like the rapture of the deer?

Section 4 (Chapters 18-21)
Word List

agonizing	astound
Audubon Society	crepuscular
extinction	insurance premiums
kerosene	loon
multitude	notion
pine away	rucksack
savanna	superficial
torrent	

Questions

1. What did the two zookeepers plan to do to Serena?
2. Why weren't they able to carry out their plan?
3. Explain Sam's plan for Louis and Serena.
4. Why did Sam want to work in the zoo?
5. How are birds and people different when it comes to money?
6. When Louis finally came home, he gave something to his father. What?
7. What did Louis's father plan to do in Billings?
8. What did the storekeeper do to Louis's father?
9. Why did the warden think that he should get to keep the money?
10. What did the storekeeper do with the money that was left over?
11. Name three places that Louis took his family when they went on vacation.
12. Where did Louis and Serena live in the summer?
13. Describe what Sam did every night before going to bed.

Writing Assignment

Sam kept a diary to help him remember what happened each day. His diary also included questions that he wanted to answer.

Pretend you are keeping a diary. Try to remember everything that happened today, and then write a paragraph for your diary. Make sure your paragraph includes a question for which you don't know the answer. If you want, you can also write a paragraph about yesterday.